THE COMPLETE GUIDE TO

RECYCLING AT HOME

THE COMPLETE GUIDE TO

RECYCLING AT HOME

How to Take Responsibility, Save Money, and Protect the Environment

GARY D. BRANSON

BETTERWAY PUBLICATIONS, INC.
WHITE HALL, VIRGINIA

Published by Betterway Publications, Inc.
P.O. Box 219
Crozet, VA 22932
(804) 823-5661

Cover design and photograph by Susan Riley
Typography by Park Lane Associates

Branson, Gary D.
The complete guide to recycling at home : how to take responsibility, save
money, and protect the environment / Gary D. Branson.
        p. cm.
    Includes index.
    ISBN 1-55870-189-3 (pbk.) : $14.95
    1. Recycling (Waste, etc.) 2. Home economics. I. Title.
TD794.5.B7 1991
363.72'82--dc20   90-21380
                                                               CIP

Printed in the United States of America
0 9 8 7 6 5 4 3 2

To my mother, Opal Branson (1907-1990),
who made a difference.

Acknowledgments

Our thanks to Bob Hostage, Hilary Swinson,
Jackie Hostage, Tim Sams, and all the folks at Betterway.

Contents

Introduction

Alexis de Tocqueville, a French historian and philosopher, toured the United States in 1831-32. After he had viewed the country, his hosts asked him what had impressed him most. De Tocqueville replied: "The magnificent waste!"

The U.S. census in 1830 counted 13 million souls. Westward expansion had not yet begun. De Tocqueville, author of *Democracy in America*, was speaking of the violence on the land of a relative handful of people. The U.S. totals about one billion, nine hundred million acres, which were originally 40 percent primeval timber, 40 percent grasslands or prairie, and 20 percent deserts or mountains. By 1945 the virgin forest area had been reduced to less than 7 percent of our land area. The forests were either logged to build a nation, or burned and cleared for farmland, in much the same way that South American rain forests are being burned today.

Today, following the twentieth observance of Earth Day, the waste is considerably more magnificent. The enormity of the waste problem is due in large part to the fact that our population has grown to an estimated 250 million people, or almost twenty times as large as in the 1830s. Dr. Paul Erhlich warned us in his book *The Population Bomb* (Rivercity Press, 1971), that we were rapidly becoming overcrowded, and that we were beginning to place severe strains upon the environment.

When World War II ended in 1945 the U.S. population was about 133 million people. The current estimate for the 1990 census is 250 million people, or a population growth of about 120 million people over the last forty-five years.

Consider the population growth, then consider that each of us contributes about 3½ pounds of waste to the pile *each day*, for a total generation of about 1200 pounds of waste per person, per year. Unless we take control of the situation it will certainly get worse: each decade several thousand new products appear on supermarket shelves. There are spray cans filled with chemicals we didn't know we needed, disposable diapers, electrical gadgets, and single-item packaging, to name but a few recent arrivals.

LET GEORGE DO IT

In addition to the burgeoning population growth there is a distressing tendency to blame all our problems on the other person, the other political party, the next level of government. How human it is to summon the scapegoat and, like Aaron in the Old Testament, lay the symbolic sins of the people on its head and banish it into the wilderness. Unfortunately, as my southern friends often observe, "That dog (or goat) won't hunt." We the people are the problem.

In his book, *Our Plundered Planet* (Little, Brown

& Co., 1948), Fairfield Osborne wrote that ecological damage is "... the story of human energy unthinking and uncontrolled. No wonder there is this new concept of man as a large-scale geological force ..." Osborne realized that man the consumer is not the entire problem. In addition to our roles as individual citizens, we (*not they*) run or work for those "big business" corporations that are attacked as undesirable citizens. We build the cars and repair them, we design and build the houses, we own and work for the public utilities. We must face up to the truth if we are to solve the problem, and the truth is, as Pogo once observed, "We have met the enemy, and he is us."

A recent article on the garbage crisis in *Audubon* magazine quoted Janet Green, a botanist who is a member of the citizen board of the Minnesota Pollution Control Agency. She said: "It boils down not so much to a garbage crisis as a crisis in individual responsibility. The public assumes it's a government problem when it's really an individual problem. ... We need people to accept responsibility for their own wastes ..."

THE *EXXON VALDEZ*

If we are serious about cleaning up the pollution, what might one assume would be a fair and just penalty for the oil spill in Alaska? Before we set too harsh a penalty, we might consider the information in the March issue of *Learning '90*. That issue noted that oil carelessly dumped by consumers (used oil from automobile, lawn, and recreational equipment) is equal in volume to *twenty or more* spills by the *Exxon Valdez*, on an annual basis. That consumers spread their gooey mess over a larger area makes it no less polluting. Even if proven the result of carelessness, the tanker spill was still an accident, whereas our own oil spills

are done with reckless intent. Or consider that windows that are poorly fitted or weatherstripped leak more energy (cumulatively) each year than the total output of the North Slope oil fields. Or we might ponder the fact that the Congress sternly pointing the finger at Exxon voted to bring North Slope oil out by tanker, rather than opting for a trans-Canada pipeline.

We might also consider that old, poorly-tuned, and inefficient cars contribute two-thirds of our air pollution, while industry contributes an estimated 20 percent. Is there a personal, individual message in the news that the friends of the earth left behind 150 tons of trash, in New York City alone, on Earth Day?

Dan Syrek, founder of the Institute of Applied Research in Sacramento, California, surveys roadside litter along state, local, or federal streets and highways. Syrek reports that he found highways in the South Bronx and a portion of Interstate 80 in San Francisco tied in the amount of junk drivers threw from autos: they were tied at *40,000 pieces of litter per mile*. Syrek observes that there is no question of the source of the problem: drivers in this country are litterbugs who toss trash from their car windows. He also found that, in cold climates, litter rates double when the temperature climbs from 50° to 70°. Various government agencies hire Syrek not only to survey the amount, but also the source, of the litter thrown. Soon your government will be able to target those companies whose packaging contributes most to roadside litter, and perhaps we can reduce the amount by changing the packaging.

The good news is that we are not beyond redemption: the state of Texas is cited as having a good record and clean highways. Perhaps the Texas results are the result of Lady Bird Johnson's campaign to beautify the highways; perhaps it was drivers' fear of the threat: Don't Mess with Texas!

CONCLUSION

My point is to consider that cleaning up our environment is the duty of us all. And we must act individually first. Pointing the finger of blame at the other political party, or the other organization, or business or industry has missed and will miss the point. While looking for something else I opened *The College Anthology* (Scott, Foresman and Company, 1945). There I found a section titled "Problems of the modern world" with a subchapter titled "Environment." The text is one I studied at Friends University (in Wichita, Kansas) in 1952. Concern for our environment is not new, which may come as a shock to the young among us. I was in my twenties (thirty years ago) when the Ohio River caught fire and was declared a fire hazard. Our problem is that the individual has waited for the government to solve the problem; the government periodically issues warning to industry, while the problem gets worse and the decades pass.

While thinking about writing this book the fall season came to Minnesota, and I removed more than eighty bags of leaves from my lawn. It costs me $25 per month to have my trash hauled away. It costs many more dollars to buy potting soil (which I could make myself by mulching my grass clippings) and for fertilizer treatments for the lawn to replace the nutrients removed when I bagged the grass.

We have unthinkingly drifted, or have been led, into a wasteful and polluting lifestyle. As a child in the Depression the motto was "Use it up, wear it out, make it do, then do without." Not much was wasted: grass clippings were left to return their nutrients to the soil; worn clothes were cut up and made into the now-expensive bed quilts; a discarded tire became a child's swing.

My point is that not only can the individual make a difference, he or she is the only one who *can* make a difference. Collectively, our buying decisions, our "lifestyles," are the deciding factor. Further, to reduce the waste flow by half is really a fairly simple thing to do, if we all cooperate. And, if my latest utility bill is any indication, it will be in our financial best interests to do our recycling at home, through buying decisions and the way we handle our home waste. Finally, someone said during Earth Week that "We did not inherit the Earth from our parents; we borrowed it from our children." I like that.

In the employees' lounge of a local store I spotted this sign: "If you mother isn't coming over later to tidy up, please clean up your own mess." We could cancel all concerned government agencies if everyone would just read — and heed — Robert Fulghum's book, *All I Really Need to Know I Learned in Kindergarten* (Villard Books, 1989): "If you make a mess, clean it up."

1
Precycling

Most governmental agencies refer to environmental shopping as "source reduction." But in San Francisco Maureen O'Rorke, owner of Maureen O'Rorke Public Relations and Advertising, has coined a new and better word for it: *precycling*. Precycling or source reduction refers to the way each and every one of us can affect the waste stream by making environmentally sound buying decisions. These buying decisions are based on several premises.

First, we can choose products that are in themselves environmentally preferable. In this area Ms. O'Rorke points out that "real lemon" cleaning power can be had if you use juice squeezed from a real lemon, rather than using lemon-scented aerosol sprays. In the same manner, one might consider an open window to be an air freshener preferable to a spray product, and a fly swatter might be a safer option to packaged bug sprays. Second, we can choose to avoid those products that we can easily live without: electric knives, can openers, and other such small appliances are examples. Finally, we can choose to buy those products that offer the most conservative (in bulk) and recyclable packaging. This may mean buying the "large economy size" to avoid buying many small packages, or choosing aluminum cans over plastic bottles if we have aluminum recycling facilities in our area but do not have facilities for recycling plastic. Or we can shop the farmers'

market and buy our vegetables in bulk, and also bring a bag from home to tote our purchases away, rather than buying the two tomatoes-per-foam-tray offerings commonly found at supermarkets.

Manufacturers are highly sensitive to all our buying decisions. Consumers, if united, can change the flow of waste considerably if we reward those who are most environmentally aware in their packaging, and punish those who create packaging simply as a marketing tool and say to hell with the environment. But we must keep abreast of studies that are being and will be done, to be sure our opinions are based on fact. For example: Many consumers consider that buying glass bottles is the superior choice over buying aluminum cans or plastic bottles. But are we sure that collecting, hauling, and washing beverage or food containers of glass is less damaging to the environment than are plastic throwaways? There are no apparent free rides to be had environmentally: every product, every container, has a downside cost as well as having environmental pluses. As noted in Chapter 4, "Plastics," plastic packaging has made real contributions to our society in lessening product cost, and in reducing the weight and mass of the trash generated. Everyone has an agenda, and our most difficult task may be trying to sort out the truth, because environmental groups are pursuing your dollar, just as manufacturers are, and exaggeration is seen on both sides.

OVER-PACKAGING

It is estimated that of every $11 we spend for groceries, one dollar is for packaging. Packaging accounts for fully one-half of household waste volume, according to the WorldWatch Institute in Washington, DC.

Let me give you an example. Yesterday I made a trip to my local home center to buy a toilet tank (flush) lever. The desired item was in a blister pack card, and the card was at least four times as wide as the flush lever. When I laid out the necessary money to pay for the lever the cashier put this single item in a plastic bag, then pushed a sales catalog into the bag unasked. The fact was that I had visited the store the day before, I already had a copy of the sales catalog, and I didn't want or need a bag to carry this single item home. The waste generated by this simple transaction was absolutely remarkable, and it is easy to see why our daily activities, when multiplied by the millions of individuals who are shopping, produce a mountain of trash.

In fairness to the manufacturer, let us recognize that this sort of packaging was until recently taken for granted, so we can hardly blame the manufacturer for selling us what we so eagerly and mindlessly buy. But with the heightened awareness of the mess we are creating, most manufacturers are becoming sensitive to the waste they produce and many are trying to act responsibly.

An example of environmental concern by a manufacturer might be Procter and Gamble's recent move to package their fabric softener (Downy) in small, concentrated amounts. The idea is that the shopper will buy one full-size, 64 oz. jug and then buy paperboard containers of the concentrate. When he runs out of softener, he mixes a carton of concentrate with water, thus reducing the number of 64 oz. size plastic bottles. Will the consumer applaud this move and buy the concentrate, or are we so concerned with convenience that we will let the product languish on the shelves? Many such household products could be packaged in concentrated form, thus reducing the number of containers generated while reducing the energy needed to haul water across country, the extra weight in the larger container being pure water.

Manufacturers freely admit that much of the oversized packaging is designed to present an advertising billboard to the passing customer, and to bulk up one product to squeeze out competitors. The consumer should complain of large boxes that are only two-thirds full of product, whether the product is cornstarch or corn flakes.

Another easy step to reduce packaging is to carry your own bags or other containers when shopping, and avoid takeout bags from the grocer or other businessman. As I have noted elsewhere, in the Depression days of the '30s each householder folded his own canvas shopping bag under an arm when going shopping. The practice was abandoned when stores began stocking an endless supply of paper bags, and now plastic bags are becoming more popular.

Consumers could help reduce the trash flow by carrying their own bags, or by refusing a bag if offered one to carry a single item. Clerks, on the other hand, should be trained to ask the customer whether they need a sales catalog or brochure, and to avoid stuffing extra paper napkins and mustard, ketchup, and salt portions into fast-food bags.

HOME MAINTENANCE PRODUCTS

How many times have you ordered three quarts of paint, only to be told by the clerk that "you might as well take a gallon, it's cheaper"? That's a prime example of the way we all think: we throw things away because it is cheaper than recycling them, and that goes for auto tires, newspapers, and dried-up paint leftovers. In the case of paint, if we

Materials in the Waste Stream

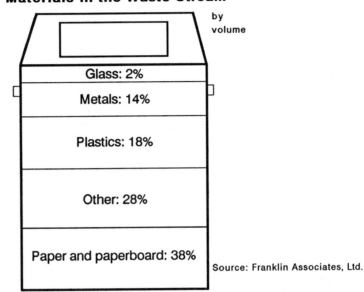

by volume

Glass: 2%

Metals: 14%

Plastics: 18%

Other: 28%

Paper and paperboard: 38%

Source: Franklin Associates, Ltd.

really only need three quarts we should not be forced to pay a cash penalty for buying only what we need. The reality is that it is more expensive for the manufacturer to package quarts, plus there is the problem of disposing of three paint cans rather than one gallon can. But the leftover paint or other chemicals is a greater problem to the environment than are the paint cans.

An enormous amount of the home products we buy ends up unused. This includes paint and attendant paint chemicals such as brush cleaners, thinners, and removers; caulk, driveway sealers, cleaning products, and adhesives or glues. Who does not have a half-tube of dried glue tucked away in a shop or kitchen drawer? To combat this problem, some manufacturers now package glues in "one-shot" tubes that hold only a small amount of glue.

To avoid leftover paint, use up the remaining paint by painting a closet, or by giving one wall of the room an extra coat of paint. Save an ounce or two of paint for touchup, but pour it into a small

jar such as a baby food jar, and clean the pail out. Oil or alkyd paint will harden in the bottom of the paint pail and you can discard it, secure in the knowledge that there is no liquid paint to ooze out and contaminate the ground in the landfill. Latex paint residue will often skim over, but the paint underneath will remain fluid, and it presents a hazard to the soil it may be buried in. Use latex paints for most applications, because latex paints are less polluting than oil or alkyd paints. Also, you can avoid buying, storing, and disposing of paint sundry items such as thinners and brush cleaners if you use latex paints exclusively. Clean brushes or rollers in hot soapy water, then rinse with clear water to remove soap and paint residue.

For jobs where only oil-base products will do, such as exterior stain products, check to be sure the product meets government standards for volatile organic compounds (VOCs). State and federal agencies are setting stricter standards for any paint product that might contribute to air quality problems.

As a magazine editor who edited a "hints" column, I was bombarded with ideas for sealing the spouts on opened caulk tubes, so the product would not dry up before it could be used. Some caulk products now come with a plastic cover for the tip; handymen often use electrical wire nuts for this purpose.

The best approach is to look around the house for other cracks that need caulking, and plan your work so you use up the entire caulk tube. Any air that contacts unused caulk or tube-type adhesives will cause the material to harden and clog the spout, so you cannot use any leftovers at a future date.

YARD MAINTENANCE

Some of the most potent products we use around the home are toxic products for the lawn and garden. Fertilizers, herbicides, and pesticides are all potential hazards. Not only do these products present a potential hazard to people and their pets, the chemical runoff is a potential source of water pollution. Fertilizer runoff can cause plant growth that will clog lakes and streams. In Chapter 3, "Lawn and Garden," we suggest ways to reduce the use of these chemicals, plus suggesting non-polluting options to currently accepted lawn chemicals.

In addition to lawn and garden chemicals, we propose to greatly reduce the waste flow from plastic lawn bags. Composting, mulching, and shredding all offer options to bagging lawn wastes.

CARS

Probably our most dangerous polluter is the car. If you combine the chemicals used in a car, plus the air pollution from combustion, plus the difficulty of dealing with worn-out tires, batteries, and junked cars themselves, cars become a ready tar-

get for environmental groups.

Manufacturers of fluids used in cars are becoming very conscious of the public clamor over car wastes. One new development we've just seen on TV is a machine that can be hooked to your car's radiator and will pump out the antifreeze, circulate it through a series of filters, add rust-proofing and other additives in small quantities, and return the cleaned antifreeze to your radiator for reuse. This will end the problem of how to dispose of old antifreeze, but will doubtless be a more expensive alternative than changing your own fluids.

In Chapter 7, "Cars," we discuss buying the best quality tires, batteries, and filters in order to reduce these wastes. I've had car batteries that have lasted for seven years; 72-month warranties for batteries are not uncommon. Also, buying high-mileage tires and following proper maintenance procedures for rotating, aligning, balancing, and inflating tires will extend their wear and put money in your pocket while reducing the amount of waste generated by cars.

Additives

Check any auto supply store or department store, and you will find a wide array of chemical products that promise to do wonders for your car. There are carburetor cleaners, cleaners for fuel injectors, paint cleaners, tire cleaners, engine cleaners, and window cleaners. There are products that propose to stop leaks from antifreeze, oil, transmission fluids. There are products that promise to clean valves, raise your engine's horsepower, improve acceleration, and stain-proof your upholstery. And most of these products are worthless, or at best stop-gap measures.

Before adding any product to your gas, oil, transmission fluid, or radiator, check your owner's manual and/or your car dealer. Most car manufacturers do not speak highly of automotive additive products. The best advice is to use the oil that is recommended in your owner's manual; buy good filters and have the oil changed at recommended intervals or whenever it gets dirty. To keep the carburetor or fuel injectors clean, use a major brand of gasoline, and fill with premium about every third tank. Premium gasoline is reported to contain an array of detergents that will clean out the fuel injectors and keep fuel lines clean.

If you spot a leak under your car, check to see what the fluid is. Gasoline has its telltale odor; antifreeze has the familiar red or yellow-green color; oil can be identified by smell or by rubbing it between your fingers. If there is any doubt, have your mechanic inspect the car's underside. The problem may be as simple as a loose hose clamp or a cracked radiator hose. It may be that the bolts on the pan or transmission should be tightened. Whatever the problem, don't try to solve it by using stop-leak products or additives. A car that is properly maintained will not leak fluids, should not leak fluids, and the leak is not only an expensive problem because of the need to add fluids constantly, it is a prime cause of auto pollution. Not only do you waste auto chemicals but the trash pile from all those plastic containers could annually create a ski slope. Don't use them.

Before we leave the subject of cars, we should point out that, in many snow states, cars rust out before they wear out. Moisture and salt collect under car body panels and first eat away the finish, then attack the steel. Wash your car frequently in winter if your roads are salted for ice. You'll extend the life of your car if you keep it clean.

CLEANING PRODUCTS

While working as a magazine editor I did an interview column called "Pro Advice." One of the pros I interviewed was Don Aslett, who founded a multi-million dollar cleaning business. Aslett advised (see p. 27 of *Do I Dust or Vacuum First?*) that the homeowner is offered a selection of housecleaning products that may differ only in their color or scent; that most cleaning products are made from the same basic ingredients. That being so, Aslett goes on to suggest that the average homeowner really needs only three types of cleaners:

1. a neutral, all-purpose cleaner to be used for most housework;

2. a disinfectant cleaner where germ or odor control is necessary such as in the bathroom or sick room; and

3. for small windows that can't be squeegee'd dry, an evaporative type window cleaner. Period.

Most cleaning products that you find on supermarket shelves are very dilute, not concentrated. The consumer pays dearly for products that are in fact merely a few ounces of chemical, packaged with a gallon of water. We pay millions in extra costs for packaging and transporting that water.

Aslett contends that all cleaning products will one day be available concentrated and contained in small foil packages. Until that happy day, Aslett recommends that the consumer buy concentrated cleaner products from a janitors' supply house, add water to dilute the cleaner to usable proportions, and pour that mix into your own reusable spray bottles. The spray bottles also are available at your janitors' supply store. A warning: Don't use more chemical than directed in an attempt to be your own chemist and create your own "super" cleaner. Just follow the manufacturer's suggested proportions to have a highly effective cleaning solution. In addition to doing the environment a favor, Aslett suggests that buying the concentrated products can save you as much as 75 percent on cleaning supplies.

Aslett also points out that most of the wood-care products sold for use on cabinets, paneling, and the like, have no beneficial effect on wood. If the wood product has a urethane or varnish finish, no product can penetrate the finish to renew, revitalize, or otherwise affect the wood. Just use your favorite cleaning product, or ask the janitors' supply dealer to suggest a cleaning product for you.

To reduce your demand for chemical cleaners, and at the same time reduce cleaning chores by many hours per month, do two simple things. First, put business-sized door mats at all entry doors. Most of the dirt that enters your house is brought in on your shoes, so door mats mean less dirt in the house. Next, buy and replace your forced-air furnace filters monthly during the heating season (and during the summer season if you also have central air conditioning).

The blower motor on your furnace can become a dust machine if you let filters get clogged with dirt. Dirt blown through heating ducts dirties walls, ceiling, drapes, and furniture, and increases the need for cleaning and decorating products.

Smoking

As a former chain smoker of cigarettes, I try very hard to avoid preaching to others on the subject of smoking. But as a former painting contractor I must tell you that a major source of my painting income I owed to homeowners who dirtied their homes with cigarette smoke. A painter can easily tell if the residents of a house are smokers by inspecting the color of the ceilings. If the ceilings are a dirty nicotine-yellow you are in a smoker's house. If you are dubious about how cigarette smoke can dirty a ceiling, hold up something that is truly white, such as a piece of typing paper, against your ceilings. You will be surprised at how yellow your ceilings really are, when you can see them in contrast to white. Next, not only did we repaint smokers' ceilings twice as often, it was also more expensive. The yellow from nicotine will bleed right through the water-base spray materials and turn the new finish yellow. To prevent this, we first had to apply an alkyd-base sealer to stop nicotine from bleeding through the finish coat. It may be, if nicotine cannot be sealed in with paint,

that it is not good for your lungs. In any event, if you smoke, you can add the cost of redecorating your home to the other costs of smoking.

BATTERIES

In the past weeks I have replaced batteries in my wristwatch, my 6-volt lantern, Fish-Lo-K-Tor, travel alarm clock, pocket calculator, smoke alarm (3), TV remote control switch, and camera (a button battery for the light meter, plus two AA batteries for the flash attachment). This is true despite the fact that I try to avoid products that are battery-powered. Factor in the additional problem of batteries for toys, for families with children, and you have a tremendous battery load on our waste stream.

What can you do about the battery glut? First, consider buying products that do not require batteries. Next, consider buying rechargeable batteries instead of the more common disposable batteries. And finally, dispose of batteries properly.

Flashlight batteries are usually either alkaline or carbon-zinc cells. These two types contain little mercury and are usually just discarded in the trash. (Check whether your community has a battery recycling program; many communities do.)

Button batteries used in cameras, watches, and the like contain some silver and mercury and can be recycled. Some drug and camera stores that sell these batteries are involved in recycling them — check where you buy your batteries. Battery manufacturers, in response to pressure from some states and groups, are working to reduce the amount of mercury used in batteries. Look for batteries that are marked "Low mercury" or ask your dealer to handle only low-mercury batteries.

Try not to store batteries for collection. They can be a hazard to inquisitive children who can swallow the batteries, or insert them in nose or ears. Instead, remove the old battery at home and take it along so you can be sure:

1. that you are buying the proper replacement battery, and

2. that you can dispose of the battery where you buy the replacement, assuming the dealer has a recycling program.

DISPOSABLE DIAPERS

When I was raising a family we bought cotton diapers by the dozen and laundered them at home. Today, the disposable diaper has become a $3.8 billion per year business. While they are a boon to parents, disposable diapers are now under attack because they clog landfills with tons of debris and human excrement. Increasingly, environmentalists are urging a return to cloth diapers.

However, the people who make disposable diapers point out that the energy needed to launder cloth diapers, plus the fuel used in diaper service vehicles, is a larger problem for the environment than are the disposable diapers. Plus, manufacturers promise that they are close to offering diapers that are biodegradable. The debate rages on, while young parents continue to opt for the convenience of disposables, and most day care facilities require that parents supply disposable diapers, so parents are in a quandary.

A major objection to disposable diapers is that they contain human excrement, which is known to harbor all sorts of germs and disease-causing viruses. Manufacturers suggest that parents rinse the disposables in the toilet to remove the waste before discarding the diapers.

It is unlikely that any degradable diaper will be found, because the degrading process requires air and water to occur. Landfills are designed to prevent any degradation of buried materials, and special precautions are taken to avoid penetration of the refuse by water or air.

It would appear that the best solution is to return to cloth diapers, home-laundered. This approach avoids the use of energy to pick up and return the diapers by a commercial diaper service, but requires energy and detergent use for the home laundry. An option would be to rinse human wastes from the disposable diapers before discarding them. Least desirable would be to continue as we have for the past twenty years, discarding the diapers and their contents into landfills that are laughingly called "sanitary landfills." It is of course remotely possible that technology can yield some product that will actually degrade when it is placed in the landfill, but no such product is yet apparent in the market.

NON-POLLUTING PRODUCTS

The most sensible products are those that can be used either with no damage to the environment, products that have already been recycled, or products, such as mulching mowers and composters, that can be used to help reduce the waste flow. In the Appendix is a beginner's list of companies that make products that fit one or more of the mentioned categories. Among those listed are companies that have furnished information or direction for this book, or whose corporate purpose is to offer non-polluting products. The list is not comprehensive, nor is it meant to be.

For those whose concern does not stop with self-interest, solving their own disposal problems, or reducing their own disposal costs, companies are springing up almost daily to try to meet the demand for cleaner, safer products. We urge readers to watch for these companies in their own communities. Check with local government offices for businesses in your town or state that offer environmentally safe products. Keep in mind, that each cause brings forth its quota of rip-off artists, ready to profit from your legitimate concerns.

To reduce successfully the amount of waste we

generate, it is useful to know what products make up the largest percentages of the waste stream. Paper and paperboard products comprise more than one-third of landfill wastes, at 35.6 percent. Next in line, by sheer tonnage, are yard wastes at 20.1 percent of the waste. Next, and about equal in their contribution, are metals, food, glass, and plastics, each around 8 percent.

It should be apparent that those products that have been the greatest offenders are, happily, the most easily recycled. In the case of yard wastes, we will show how to reduce them to almost zero by better lawn and garden management.

As our landfills become filled to capacity, cities are refusing to accept any yard wastes at all and urging recycling and source reduction in other waste materials. By sorting, handling, and wise shopping for other materials we can improve the recovery rate and clean up the country.

CHECKLIST

PRECYCLING

❑ Check out which materials are being recycled in your area before making buying choices; i.e., cut down on buying glass-packaged products if glass recycling is unavailable.

❑ Consider how you will dispose of waste of any product you buy.

❑ Reject over-packaged products or complain to the manufacturer. Remember, about 50 percent of the waste stream from residences is packaging.

❑ Buy concentrated products and add your own water.

❑ Bring your own shopping bags.

❑ When possible, buy non-toxic products (see Chapter 3).

❑ Buy only as much product as you need and use up all you buy.

❑ Avoid using products of questionable effectiveness, such as additives for motor oil or gasoline.

❑ Replace furnace filters monthly to keep air and furnishings clean. Better still, install an electronic air cleaner.

❑ Don't smoke. Tobacco smoke is a primary indoor air pollutant; it increases frequency and cost of cleaning, decorating.

❑ Buy refillable pump applicators rather than aerosol dispensers.

❑ Buy rechargeable batteries for most uses. Look for and buy low mercury batteries when possible.

❑ Use cotton diapers and wash them yourself. When disposable diapers are necessary, rinse feces from diapers before disposing of them.

❑ Buy quality products and take care of them to reduce your cost of living as well as reducing the waste stream.

❑ Save all owner's manuals and study care and maintenance instructions.

❑ Don't get mad, get a refund. Return shoddy merchandise to discourage purveyors of junk.

❑ Check with test publications such as *Consumer Reports* before buying. Learn to buy on a basis of "life cycle costing," considering initial cost, yearly maintenance and operating costs, and estimated years of service.

❑ Sell or donate cast-off clothes, don't trash them.

❑ Lobby your state legislature for enforcement of litter laws on highways.

2
Paper

With all the fuss about waste disposal, many people are still not aware that the greatest problem is paper. Paper and paperboard products account for about 37 percent of landfill wastes, by weight. By the same token, paper is among the leaders in waste recycling: 24 million tons, or 29 percent of waste paper, was recycled in 1987, and that rate is increasing. It is estimated that 50 million Americans are involved in waste paper collection and recycling.

So why is paper a landfill problem? Why don't we just recycle all the waste paper and end the problem? The answer is that there are more than fifty kinds of waste paper, and these different kinds of paper can be recycled only to a limited extent.

The key is the consumer: if we are to recycle the paper we must return it in recyclable form. That means we should not mix various kinds of paper together, making it difficult to sort. In addition to sorting the paper we must keep it clean, and free of food wastes or other contamination.

DISPOSING OF PAPER WASTE

For paper, as for all wastes, we have four choices for disposing of waste.

1. Waste reduction means we can reduce the amount of paper generated, either by using less paper, or taxing or imposing deposits on various products.

2. We can recycle paper products for reuse.

3. For products that cannot be recycled, we can burn them in waste-to-energy incinerators, using the heat generated to create steam or electricity and thus salvage energy from the waste.

4. Last and least desirable, we can dispose of paper wastes in landfills.

There are seventy waste/energy plants in the U.S., with another thirty plants under construction or being planned. Recycling does the following:

*   provides a fiber source for paper mills;

*   income to collectors, dealers, and processors;

*   reduces disposal costs and saves space in landfills (a ton of waste paper takes up 3.3 cubic yards of space);

*   helps reduce our U.S. balance of trade when sold overseas.

We have a current goal of recovering 40 percent of waste paper by 1995, a goal that should be possible. Paper collection efforts during World War II, for example, reached a utilization rate of 35.3 percent. There are 600 paper and paperboard mills in the U.S.; 200 of these mills use recycled paper exclusively, while others in varying amounts.

Many companies that package their products in recycled paper-board use the recycling symbol to indicate that the carton is made from recycled paper.

Companies producing paper products that are recyclable use the reverse of this symbol.

To understand the figures for recycling, and what level would represent a reasonable goal, we must understand how paper is used. The U.S. consumed 83 million tons of paper and paperboard products in 1987. Of that amount, 23.2 million tons were recovered for recycling. Nine million tons of paper went for permanent uses: books, permanent files, and for construction use. Six million tons of paper were unrecoverable: toilet paper, cigarette papers, papers burned or used in rural areas where there was no recovery system. Forty-five million tons were discarded into municipal solid waste systems or landfills. Thus twice as much paper was lost in landfills as was recovered.

UNDERSTANDING PAPER

How can the consumer reduce this 45 million tons of buried paper? First, we must understand what makes paper unacceptable for recycling. Regardless of any "recyclable" claims you may see printed on fast food containers, paper that is soiled with food or grease cannot be recycled. The food contaminants attract insects and rodents, and develop offensive odors. Be aware that food chains that so mark their containers are being dishonest with you: the paper product may be recyclable *until* they put food in it, but not after. By the same token, we must avoid dumping the paper into the garbage container where it can become soiled with grease, food scraps, or coffee grounds. Such paper is lost for recycling. (Paper that is soiled can be burned for energy at incinerators.)

Paper that has been "processed" — that is, coated with wax, or laminated to foil — is difficult to recover. Also a problem for recycling is pressure-sensitive adhesives used to bind products such as magazines together, hot-melt adhesives used to bind phone books, and any adhesive that is not water soluble.

Office waste paper is high quality but also has staples, inks, and other coatings that must be re-moved at the mill. However, these high-grade office papers are worth more, and are separated out to become "sorted white ledger," a valuable resource.

A problem for recyclers of waste paper is how to create a steady demand that will keep processing plants busy. As one might suspect, waste paper demand is highest in boom times; when business slows, so slows the demand for waste paper. Another problem is that cellulosic fibers break down in recycling. Fiber cannot be endlessly recycled, and new fibers must be added with each reuse.

What becomes of recycled paper? Of the 24 million tons of paper recovered in 1987, 4.2 million tons were exported to countries that are short on forests and fiber. Paper experts expect this foreign demand to continue, and to grow. Five hundred thousand tons of waste paper were converted to products such as cellulosic insulation, packing/cushioning products, and molded pulp products such as egg cartons or cafeteria food trays. Recycling newspapers earned $100 million dollars in annual income, with another $100 million earned by those who collect cardboard (corrugated) boxes. In 1987, 40 percent of corrugated boxes were recovered.

USE LESS PAPER

Can we reduce the paper glut by using less paper? I recall a story from our first energy crisis, in which the U.S. government workers in Washington, DC were asked to make suggestions on how to reduce the mountain of paper used by the government. The suggestions came flowing back to the supervisors, printed on tons and tons of paper.

One major source of waste paper is from newspapers. Should newspapers take the lead in reducing their own contribution to the trash flow? Out of curiosity, while preparing this book, I saved all my newspapers for a month. I take a daily paper, plus the Sunday jumbo edition. At the end of the month I weighed the papers: I had collected 30 pounds of newspapers for the month, or about one pound per day. Could the paper carriers (for a small additional fee) follow the lead of auto parts outlets, and pick up yesterday's paper when they deliver today's? Could the newspapers cut their total output of paper by printing two editions, one of which was the usual news/classified package, the other paper being the news only, with the classified section omitted? Many times we discard the classified section unread. I know this approach presents a problem for the newspapers, which depend for their income on advertising revenue. Obviously, ad revenue is based on the number of readers who are exposed to the advertisement. But the newspapers should take a part in solving the waste problem they help to create, just as those auto dealers who sell oil must provide (or direct the customer to) a disposal site for used oil. It is not enough that newspapers simply propose to use more recycled paper.

A second source of waste paper for homeowners is magazines. I have been a magazine editor, and still write editorials for some magazines. Again, circulation managers and publishers might not look kindly on the idea, but I think that magazines should be read by the greatest number of people, a readership called "pass-along" in the business. Options for making magazines work harder include passing your used copies (immediately, while the information is still fresh) to your local hospital, dentist's waiting room, school or church library, or to jails and prisons.

Most paper dealers will not accept magazines if they are mixed with newsprint, so when it is time to dispose of your magazines, you should bundle them separately.

An early memory of my childhood was seeing my grandmother take her canvas shopping bag from a hook behind the door and set off grocery shopping. The canvas bags of the day were sturdy, and had double handles, like the shopping bags seen today. They were stronger, no doubt because they were often lugged home on foot, and flimsy handles would have given way, as they do today. Today, I often reach home with a half-dozen paper grocery bags to show for a weekly shopping trip for two people. It is a good day if I don't split at least one bag and spill its contents before I can get it to the kitchen.

Why did we give up the canvas shopping bags? No doubt it was more convenient to pop into the store and lug our purchases to the car. Because we don't walk to shopping we don't need a heavy bag with reinforced handles. But it would be a boon to the ecology if we would return to the old reusable bags. As an alternative, my supermarket sells heavy corrugated boxes that have handles die-cut into the ends, but the common practice is to bag the groceries and set the bags into the boxes. Or we might empty our paper grocery bags and then put them into the car trunk, to be reused for our next shopping trip. Remember, it takes one fifteen-year-old tree to make 700 grocery bags.

Paper grocery bags can also be reused — and then recycled — if we use them to hold old newspapers. Just fold the newspapers in half and tuck them into a grocery bag. This will save having to bundle the papers, will keep them separated from garbage that might soil them, and the paper bag can be recycled along with the newsprint.

Other uses for paper grocery bags include filling them with wood scraps from the workshop, or twigs and limbs from the yard, and using them for fireplace starters. The bags ignite easily to start the fire, and prevent making a mess from dropping bark, sawdust, or chips. The bags of kindling or charcoal briquets also can be taken along on fishing or camping trips or picnics, and used to start a campfire.

JUNK MAIL

At least half the daily contents of my mailbox is junk mail that comes unbidden to my door. I have seen estimates that we could heat several hundred thousand homes each year with the junk mail that is generated by the growing number of mailing lists in this country.

Your name is a valuable commodity that is sold on a regular basis. Organizations survey the demographics of their members and then offer their membership lists for sale to other businesses. Magazines sell their subscription lists as a source of revenue. For example, the home magazines can sell their subscribers' names to a variety of other businesses including other magazines in the same field, mail order houses, book clubs, and others.

Most businesses and magazines post notices that they sell customer lists, but will refrain from doing so if you ask that your name be deleted. If you don't like the junk mail you receive, notify the person/company that sent the mail, and most will take your name off their lists. If you get catalogs or solicitations from companies that offer goods or services you are not and will not be interested in, advise them that they are wasting their time. Reputable companies do not wish to harass you, nor do they wish to waste their money by soliciting business from those who will never be customers. A good example might be the nurseryman who sold you tulip bulbs when you lived in a private home. He cannot know, unless you advise him, that you now live in a high-rise apartment and have no need for tulip bulbs. Ask him to delete your name from his customer list.

If you request your name be taken off a mailing list but you continue to receive junk mail, repeat your request, or advise the local postal inspector to stop the mail. If you'd like to keep your name off new mailing lists notify:

The Direct Marketing Association
6 E. 43rd Street
New York, NY 10017

While we're on the subject of unwanted junk, I often marvel at the businesses who drop flyers on my yard/walk/drive/porch, and then expect that I would ever consider doing business with them. Young carriers frequently attach junk ads to my wrought iron railing, using rubber bands, and I harvest this junk as though it were a noxious garden. I never do business with anyone who would litter my yard.

Another tip: If political candidates and their supporters had any sense, they would stop dropping those infernal political messages on our lawns. I learned this lesson years ago, while campaigning for a friend. As I crossed a lawn to deposit my campaign literature I was met by a sullen homeowner who was carrying a plastic trash bag. "Just drop it in here," was his weary request, and when I looked into the bag I saw it was full of other candidates' literature. A question to the politicos: Do you really think a citizen will vote for you when he reaches to pick trash off his lawn and sees your smiling face on the litter? If you are a candidate, or a volunteer, or a businessman seeking business, consider the impact your brochures and literature have on the parade of trash, and on the citizen's opinion of you.

For further information on paper recycling, contact:

Paper Recycling
American Paper Institute
260 Madison Avenue
New York, NY 10016

CHECKLIST

PAPER

❏ Have a separate bin or box handy for sorting paper. Paper that is soiled by food or grease cannot be recycled. Dispose of soiled paper in trash; sort clean paper for recycling.

❏ Separate newspapers from magazines and slick-paper inserts.

❏ Bring your own shopping bags.

❏ Encourage companies to start "electronic" catalogs (on cable TV, for instance) rather than printing high-cost paper catalogs.

❏ Reuse any paper grocery bags. Rather than bundling and tying paper, fold newspapers and place them in an old grocery bag. They can be recycled together.

❏ Discourage "junk mail." Ask that your name be taken off mailing lists. Instruct magazines and businesses not to sell your name to other direct marketers, if you don't want to receive junk mail.

❏ Ask your local newspaper to aid in setting up recycling facilities for newspapers.

❏ Write to manufacturers to discourage them from using oversized packaging as "billboards" to grab attention. Close to 10 percent of your food bill is for packaging.

❏ Cut old sheets and other fabric into washable rags. Use rags or reusable sponges rather than paper towels for most home cleaning chores.

❏ Lobby your political party to reduce the waste of political pamphlets and brochures.

3
Lawn and Garden

As I watched the truckers load forty bags of leaves from my lawn last fall (forty bags was less than half the total leaf output I finally disposed of), I suddenly recalled falls from the past. In those years we never generated so much lawn and garden waste. Leaves were burned, which is now illegal. Grass clippings were left to return their nutrients to the lawn; garden waste was composted or plowed under the soil. Today, we are told that between 25 and 50 percent of the waste volume in landfills is from yard wastes. How — and when — did we adopt this wasteful practice?

I put in a call to a friend who has worked for years in the lawn machinery and equipment field. How did it become accepted practice to bag and haul away lawn wastes? Don't golf courses, with the finest turf in the community, return grass clippings to the soil? Why don't golf courses bag their autumn leaves for the landfill?

My friend's response was simple. He opined that at some point, years ago, a power mower manufacturer decided to "one-up" the competition by offering a grass bagger on his lawn mowers. The competition saw sales slipping and decided to match the offer with a bagger of their own.

Grass catchers became a standard in the industry. Homeowners became accustomed to the manicured look for lawns, and we all adopted the practice of bagging lawn and garden wastes for dumping. Makers of plastic bags were enthusiastic at

this turn of events, and started making large plastic bags to hold the waste. When the clipped lawns turned brown, the chemical manufacturers obliged us with fertilizers to replace the nutrients lost when the clippings were hauled away. Waste disposal firms welcomed the extra business, as did the landfill operators who were paid for the dumping. Somehow, without meaning to, without even noticing the change, bagging and hauling lawn wastes grew to be accepted practice and good business.

Twenty or more states have legislated an end to dumping lawn wastes, and more states will soon follow. Landfill areas are quickly becoming overloaded: it is estimated that at least half of our 16,400 landfills will be closed — full to capacity — by the turn of the century.

To combat this trend, and to profit from it, the waste haulers are selling red tags priced from $1 and up. The tags must be attached to any trash bag that contains lawn or garden wastes. This refuse must be bagged separately from all other refuse, and a separate fee is charged for such lawn wastes. The fee of $1 or more per bag is the "tipping fee" for each trash bag, such bag not to exceed 50 pounds of lawn waste.

The are quite a few problems with bagging wastes. First of all, John Deere, Inc. experts claim that letting grass clippings lie on the lawn is beneficial to the grass; the opposite approach is to say that removing the clippings is detrimental to your lawn. Nutrients in the clipped grass can be the equivalent of one application of lawn fertilizer, so leaving clippings saves the manufacture and application of commercial fertilizer. Leaving the grass clippings also eliminates the need for plastic lawn bags, and for hauling the refuse to the landfill, and saves the space the materials would occupy in the landfill.

In self defense, if not for the sake of the ecology, the homeowner must reduce or eliminate yard and garden materials from the waste stream. This is not difficult to do; it just requires a bit more thought and attention than bagging the waste. The first step is to reduce waste materials to a minimum, and the second step is to handle the waste so that the yard utilizes all the vegetable material that it produces. With just a bit more thought and careful management we can reduce the yard and garden waste to zero, and we can reduce our own yard work in the process. It is both cheaper and easier to handle yard wastes at home than to package and ship them to landfills.

GETTING A HEALTHY LAWN

To reduce yard waste and to reduce the need for pesticides and fertilizers, the first step is to establish a healthy lawn. A healthy lawn will resist attacks from insects and disease, making most chemicals unnecessary. A healthy lawn needs less water. The best herbicide for controlling weed growth is a thick turf that crowds out weed seeds before they can become established. A lawn that is properly fertilized will grow steadily, but slowly, so that it does not produce rapid growth and excess grass.

First, have your soil tested to be sure you have a proper pH balance. This means a pH of between 6 and 7: neither too acid nor too alkaline soil. Your local lawn center can check the pH balance for you or sell you a do-it-yourself test kit, or many state universities will provide this service through their agriculture departments. Most northern lawns require lime to bring their pH into balance, while problem lawns in the South may require the addition of sulphur. Ask your local turf experts to direct you.

If your lawn is compacted, or the soil is heavy clay, you may need to aerate the soil. You can buy or rent aerators that have pipe-like extensions which penetrate the soil so air can get at plant roots. Also, you may have to dethatch your lawn to remove ground-level root buildup. If thatch is more than one-half inch thick, dethatch the lawn, or ask a pro to do it for you. The pro may advise you to apply a top-dressing of black dirt or peat moss to loosen heavy clay soil.

Reseed bare spots in the lawn. Grass that is winterkilled on boulevards may require an application of gypsum to sweeten the soil. Gypsum is available under such trade names as Sof-N-Soil, a United States Gypsum product. Because grass is clipped before it can reseed itself, you will have to reseed the lawn periodically. If grass looks thin, bare spots are developing, or soil seems too heavy, you may want to till the lawn and start over. Add black dirt, sand, or peat moss to loosen the soil and then reseed or sod the lawn for a fresh start.

MOWING

Don't over-fertilize and force grass growth. Let the grass grow to 2 inches or more in hot or dry weather. A good rule is to keep the grass 2 inches high and mow it before it is 3 inches high. The grass clippings that are 1 inch or less in length will fall harmlessly to the soil, and will decompose to feed the standing grass. Cut the lawn when grass leaves are dry, so they do not cling to each other or to standing grass.

Mulching mowers use blade and air action to recut grass or leaves, eliminating the need to bag lawn wastes. Photo courtesy of The Toro Company.

To avoid too-long grass clippings, you can use a mulching mower. These mowers have special blades and a special deck design that helps lift the grass and cut it several times, so clippings are reduced in length and decompose more rapidly. If you already have a mower, but it is not a mulching mower, you can simply cut the grass more often to avoid longer clippings. Incidentally, many experts feel the grass will be healthier if you do not cut more than one-third the length at one time, so frequent mowing is the wisest course, rather than cutting off too much grass leaf at one cutting. And choose a mulching mower the next time you're in the market.

If you've let the grass grow too long, or a wet season or long vacation has prevented you from mowing at the right height, consider catching the clippings and composting them. Composting, which will be discussed at greater length elsewhere in this book, is definitely the second choice for handling grass clippings. The best is to save the time, work, and expense of handling the clippings at all.

THATCH

When dealers were trying to sell us mowers with grass catchers, they charged that leaving the clippings on the lawn caused thatch. In fact, thatch is the buildup of stems and grass roots that come to the surface seeking moisture or nutrients. When you water the lawn too frequently, without ever completely soaking the lawn, the roots grow to the surface where the moisture is. By the same token, frequent application of fertilizer will cause the roots to come to the surface seeking nutrients. Proper fertilizing and deep, infrequent watering will stop thatch from developing.

One sure sign of thatch is a lawn that is riddled with tunnels from night crawlers. The night crawlers can be poisoned with Diazanon, but Diazanon is one of the chemicals that is a suspected carcinogen. If you will first dethatch, then adopt the proper watering/fertilizing techniques, you will get rid of the night crawler problem, without chemicals.

FERTILIZING

Avoid using chemical fertilizers on your lawn. Natural fertilizers such as Ringer Lawn Restore combine ingredients such as bone meal and soya to reduce soil compaction. Living microorganisms in Restore also encourage root growth and reduce the amount of water the lawn needs. Lawns need two to four pounds of nitrogen per 1,000 square feet of lawn per year. Whatever kind of fertilizer you choose, read the label application instructions. Never apply fertilizer too heavily, using a higher spread rate than suggested by the manufacturer. Too much fertilizer may burn the grass, cause excessive growth and frequent mowing, and will result in a high level of fertilizer runoff into nearby streams or lakes.

Time fertilizer applications for maximum effect. Most experts agree that people may apply fertilizer too early. For maximum effect, don't apply spring fertilizer until the grass is green and starts to grow. Later application time for summer or fall may depend on where you live: call your county agricultural extension agent for advice on fertilizing in your area. Keep in mind that leaving grass clippings on the lawn will be equal, in one season, to one chemical fertilizer application.

WATERING

A healthy lawn needs about 2 inches of rain every two weeks. This recommendation includes any rain that may fall during the period, with the balance made up by watering. Leaving the clippings on your lawn helps retain moisture that might otherwise evaporate from a bare lawn. Leaving the grass 2 inches long likewise retards evaporation and reduces the need for watering.

The easiest way to be sure your lawn gets just the right amount of water is to install an automatic sprinkling system. The down side of automatic sprinklers is that they automatically water your lawn if you're away, even though it may be raining at the same time.

Lacking an automatic sprinkling system, you can easily measure the amount of water you sprinkle onto the lawn. Use several large cans, such as coffee cans, and paint markings inside the cans at 1 and 2 inch depths. Set the cans randomly about the lawn while you are running your sprinklers. Check the cans frequently and move the sprinklers when you have applied the right amount of water (maximum 2 inches).

To be sure you have watered deep enough to discourage thatch or surface root growth, wait about twelve hours after watering. Then use a screwdriver to check the water depth. If the screwdriver can be easily pushed into the soil, to at least a 6-inch depth, you can be sure that the soil is properly saturated.

When you reseed your lawn, ask your lawn dealer to suggest a deep-root, drought-resistant grass for your area. Among drought-resistant species are fescue, zoysia grass, and Bermuda grass. The current news is that more drought resistant, slow-growing grasses are on the way. Botanists are breeding grass seed that will one day require little cutting, little watering, and will thus reduce the burden of lawn waste on the environment.

MULCHING

To get rid of tree branches, brush, leaves, and garden waste, consider using a chipper/shredder. The

A chipper/shredder can reduce tree limbs, twigs, grass, and leaves for mulching or composting. Photo courtesy of Garden Way Mfg.

Mulch can be used to help retain moisture, prevent weed growth, or as an attractive ground cover for gardens.

Easy to clean fiberglass bin composters are insulated to aid in building the heat levels necessary for composting. Photo courtesy of Ringer Corp.

shredder will reduce larger lawn and garden debris to small particles that will decay more readily. Used as a chipper, the device can turn tree limbs and such into wood chips that can be used in a variety of ways around the yard.

Chippers can cut limbs into 3/4-inch chips that will break down more readily in the compost heap. For making decorative landscaping chips or mulch, select the 1-inch size chips.

Where can you use all that mulch? Tour your own yard and look at possible areas where mulch can be used. The chances are that your city-sized lot will not produce enough mulch for your yard. Possible areas include around shrubs, on banks or hard-to-mow areas, in shady places where grass won't grow, along walkways (or spread for a rustic garden path), or around the base of trees where grass might rob the tree of needed water or nutrients.

Wood chips can also be used in play areas to provide a soft landing under play equipment, or to reduce dirt on kids' shoes and clothes. Just dig a pit at least 6 inches deep under swings or other play areas, then put in 2 to 3 inches of crushed rock or gravel to provide drainage. Over the gravel spread a layer, at least 3 inches deep, of wood chips.

At the house entry, use landscape timbers to define a problem area and to make it easier to mow around beds. Use mulch to set off driftwood, rocks, or sculptures. Mulch as a background will set off plants, shrubs, trees, and flowers, providing a natural-looking contrast to the other landscape elements.

Mulch can reduce yard and garden chores such as weeding and watering. In garden areas you may want to lay down a base of landscape cloth, available at garden stores, then apply a layer of mulch over the cloth. Landscape cloth lets water flow through but provides a more complete barrier to weed growth than does mulch alone.

Using a deep mulch cover in your vegetable garden can almost eliminate the chore of weeding. It is difficult for growing weeds to find their way through the heavy mulch, and blown or fallen weed seeds cannot root in the layer of wood chips. Consider, if stooping is a problem, building raised garden beds. The raised beds can contain a lot of mulch, will provide a rich environment for growing vegetables, and with proper care will be weed-free within a few seasons.

Fall leaves, too, benefit from being shredded. A shredder will reduce leaf volume: it takes ten to twelve bags of leaves to produce one bag of shredded leaves. Leaves that are shredded, or "cracked," will break down much more rapidly than whole leaves. Whole leaves become wet and soggy, choking out the grass beneath them, and the sodden mass will still be there in the spring. A friend at John Deere Co. tells me that he shreds his fall leaves, then spreads them about 6 inches deep under a row of pines at the rear of his property. This procedure is followed each fall. By spring, after the snow and winter have done their work, the leaf residue is undetectable, lost in the layer of pine needles and cones beneath the trees. Or you can compost the leaves, but shred them first to help aid the decomposition process.

COMPOSTING

Everywhere in nature we see vegetable materials decomposing and turning back into soil. This process is aided by worms, termites, microorganisms, birds, moisture, heat, and cold, as water penetrates, is frozen and expands. This necessary part of the life cycle can be aided by controlling the conditions that promote decomposition.

As we have noted, the composting cycle is accomplished quickly and effortlessly in the case of certain materials. Grass clippings, for example, have a high nitrogen content, are fragile, and return quickly to the soil. Other vegetable materials such as tree leaves and wood have a higher carbon content, and are more difficult to break down. For these materials and others, it is necessary to establish a compost pile.

The very thought of composting may cause us some distress. Many associate composting with a messy pile of odorous vegetable matter. But composting can be accomplished in several ways, and by choosing the least offensive methods, composting can be neither time-consuming nor a source of other problems such as animal or insect infestation or odors. Remember that most of your yard wastes can be utilized without using a designated compost pile.

Grass will decompose if left on the lawn; yard leaves may break down if they are shredded and spread beneath trees or shrubs; wood wastes such as limbs can be chipped and used as a mulch. Use these ideas to dispose of as much yard and garden waste is possible, and compost only those materials that are most difficult to break down, and then only as the last resort.

Remember that composting can be done in a number of ways. Also remember that it is best to use a shredder/grinder or other shredding tool to break the yard material into smaller particles that will decay more quickly. You can rent a shredder, perhaps borrow one, or invest in a machine if your yard/garden produces enough waste to warrant the investment. The Ringer Corporation points out that tools and machines you already own may be sufficient for most shredding operations. Kitchen wastes, for example, may be run through a blender or food processor before discarding them. Do not compost animal scraps such as meat: these will cause odors and attract rodents and insects, if left in a compost pile. The lawn mower will chop grass clippings (a mulching mower is best); and the mower can also be used to shred tree leaves. Just run the mower through piles of leaves to chop them, or catch the leaves by using a grass catcher on your mower when mowing in the fall. If you have only a small amount of leaves, put them in a garbage pail and shred them with a weed whacker.

When you have gathered the material to be composted, remember that compost piles work best when they contain a combination of fine and coarse materials. The coarse materials help loosen the compost pile so that air can circulate freely

Soil surface composting refers to letting lawn and garden wastes return to the soil. The rotary tiller helps break up weed growth, blending it into the soil to return nutrients. Photo courtesy of Garden Way Mfg.

through the material, aiding the decay action. Other factors that affect speed of decomposition include the carbon/nitrogen ratio of the material being composted (the ideal ratio of carbon to nitrogen is 25:1 to 30:1); moisture levels that promote rapid decay (compost material should be about as wet as a wrung-out sponge); the temperature of the pile (microorganisms stop working at about 40° F); and mixing and turning of the material to ensure even breakdown (most piles should be turned or stirred once a week.)

Composting methods include soil surface composting, in which the waste products from lawn or garden are left to decay, spread over the lawn or garden area; bag composting, in which small amounts of grass or other plant waste are placed in a plastic bag, dampened, fertilizer or activators is added, and the bag is sealed and left until natural decomposition occurs; or gathering the composting materials into a pile that may then be enclosed in a container-type composter. The contain-er composter may be a wooden structure you can build, a wire fence enclosure, or one of the many steel or fiberglass drum composters that are now offered by yard and garden supply firms.

The type of composting you select will depend on what materials your yard and garden generates, plus the projected volume of materials to be disposed of. No matter which method you choose, remember that composting time will be greatly reduced by proper compost management. You must remember that shredding or chipping materials into smaller particles, keeping the mix damp (but not wet), maintaining proper temperatures, and turning or mixing the compost frequently all will speed decomposition and minimize composting problems such as odors and insect or animal infestation. Your rewards for this effort will be a better lawn or garden, less expense for chemicals, insecticides, and waste removal — plus the knowledge that you are doing your bit to reduce your home's impact on the environment.

Bag composting is a simple technique for small amounts of leaves or grass clippings. These kits contain plastic bags, compost maker, and instructions. Photos courtesy of Ringer Corp.

Soil Surface Composting

As the name indicates, in soil surface composting the wastes generated by the lawn or garden are simply left in place, rather than being gathered up and composted in a bin. Grass clippings on a lawn, for example, may be simply dropped and forgotten: the high nitrogen content of the grass, and the size of the fragile clippings, will ensure that they will decompose without any further effort on your part.

For gardens, take a lesson from the farmers who reap the grain but leave the leaves and stalks scattered on the fields. After harvesting the vegetables from the garden, let the plants wilt and fall onto the garden surface. You may even choose to add to this vegetation by spreading shredded leaves or bagged grass clippings over the garden surface. Experts from the Ringer Corporation point out that the layer of plant waste can be 4 to 6 inches thick for fall composting, or should be reduced to 2 to 3 inches if applied in the spring, nearer to planting time. Generally, the best time to surface compost is in the fall. Let the garden waste dry out, then turn the material into the soil with a tiller. The loosened soil, plus the mixed-in waste material, will catch and trap rain and snow. Knowledgeable farmers favor fall plowing to trap winter snow and to add nitrogen (called the "poor man's fertilizer") to the soil. Keep in mind that you should remove any diseased plants or vines from the garden to avoid the carry-over of disease.

In spring, spread a product such as Ringer Spring Garden Soil Restore over the garden, to aid waste decomposition and to free growth nutrients. When it's warm enough to plant, again till to break up the soil for a seedbed. Keep a chart of your garden, and rotate the plants annually so you're not replanting your vegetables in the same soil each season.

Bag Composting

Waste products such as grass clippings and kitchen vegetables decompose quickly, and will not yield large quantities for disposal in the well-managed home. These products are, therefore, ideal candidates for bag composting.

To compost in a plastic bag, shred the grass or vegetable wastes into fine particles. Place them in a plastic yard bag, add a cup of high-nitrogen fertilizer, and dampen the bag's contents. Don't add too much water: experts advise the compost materials should be about as damp as a wrung-out sponge. Tie the top of the plastic bag and set it where it will receive the sun's heat. Turn the bag over every few days, so the mixture will break down evenly. Within three to four months you will have a rich compost that can be used in the yard or garden.

Ringer Corporation offers a Recycling Kit that contains a bag for composting, plus a package of Compost Maker, which contains bacteria and fungi to speed the breakdown of organic matter and to add nitrogen to the resulting mulch. With this system you just place the waste in the bag, add the Compost Maker and water per directions, then tie the bag top and turn the bag frequently. The kit will treat up to 280 gallons of grass clippings, costs about $15, and promises to yield mulch in only ten to thirty days.

Compost Bins

You can build a compost bin, or pile, to process larger amounts of yard or garden wastes. If you live on a city lot, you should definitely consider building or buying a container-type composter, to avoid objections from nearby neighbors. The enclosed or container-type composter will be neater, with better odor control, than an open pile. Most popular compost bins include structures made of wood or concrete blocks, fiberglass bins that may be insulated for better thermal heat buildup, or tumbler bins such as the advertised steel drums that have turning cranks and are mounted on some sort of framework and axle arrangement.

A drum composter lets you compost large quantities and can be rotated to mix materials and speed the composting process. Photo courtesy of Garden Way Mfg.

Rich humus can be spread over the lawn or returned to the garden to loosen and enrich soil. Photo courtesy of Garden Way Mfg.

Check features of the various composters carefully: you may find that you need more than one unit to handle your own particular waste load. It is useful to have two or more compost piles "working": one pile of finished mulch to work from, another pile that is active and to which more yard waste can be added.

To speed the compost action you can add activators or inoculants, which contain microorganisms, to the waste material. For example, Ringer Corporation offers a variety of such products designed to aid the decomposition process. The chemical makeup of the activators varies, depending on the nature of the waste you will compost. Check with your dealer or the manufacturer if you're unsure of which product you need. Brown Leaf Compost Maker, Grass Clippings Compost Maker, Compost Plus, and Compost Pile Recharger are four possibilities. Compost Pile Recharger, for example, is useful for starting spring activity in a compost pile that froze in cold weather before decomposition was complete.

A properly layered compost bin will have alternate layers of coarse and fine materials, each about 8 inches thick. Keep the pile dampened, without making it soggy: a damp sponge feeling is about right. Compost that is too wet will rot rather than decay. A strong sulphur smell is an indication of over-wet compost.

Within five to six days the pile may generate interior temperatures between 140° and 165°. The temperatures not only ensure rapid decomposition, but also will destroy most weed seeds and disease organisms, thus yielding a finished mulch that is harmless but beneficial to your yard and garden.

When the pile has finished cooking it will cool and have a dark color and an earthy smell. The compost can be disposed of immediately in most cases (you may want to wait until spring to spread the compost on lawn or garden). Because most of your compost will be generated in summer, you can spread it immediately on the lawn as a top dressing, on the garden to enhance the soil, or use it for starting new plants. You can make your own potting soil by mixing compost, perlite, or sand and loam together in equal portions. Store leftover potting soil in plastic bags for future use when starting hot beds or potted plants.

Carbon Nitrogen Ratios

Ringer Corporation points out that the higher the nitrogen content of a waste material, the quicker it will decay; while yard wastes that have a high carbon ratio are slower and more difficult to break down. These ratios are shown Carbon/Nitrogen (grass clippings, for example, have a C/N ratio of 19:1), and the lower the first number in the ratio, the higher the nitrogen content and the faster the decomposition. Yard materials that most concern the homeowner and their C/N ratios are:

CARBON NITROGEN RATIOS

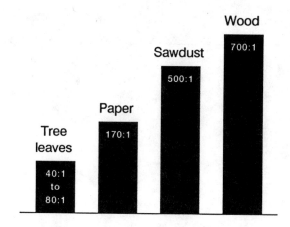

These ratios demonstrate why the materials listed are slow to decompose. By contrast, the following materials have a more favorable C/N ratio and are much easier to break down in composting:

CARBON NITROGEN RATIOS

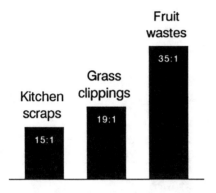

These ratios demonstrate why the addition of nitrogen to the compost mix can help improve the C/N ratio and speed decomposition, thus reducing the time needed to process the waste. The activators also cause an increase in the temperatures of the decaying matter, which is key to the speed of the process.

When the options are considered, you can see that it is possible for the homeowner to eliminate lawn and garden wastes completely from the waste stream; and not only is that possible, it can be done with a little planning and a minimum of effort. You should not be concerned that managing yard wastes might take on the dimensions of a large or time-consuming project. Recycling yard products is actually a matter of recognizing that we are really talking about changes in habit, and of realizing that this conservation is also good for your yard and your pocketbook. These simple steps, if universally adopted, would eliminate 20 percent — up to 50 percent in the growing season — of the waste materials sent to the landfills.

HERBICIDES AND PESTICIDES

A healthy lawn requires less water, less chemical fertilizer, fewer pesticides and herbicides. A thick, healthy turf growing from soil that has a proper pH balance and is loose enough to hold air, moisture, and nutrients will grow a thick stand of grass that will resist weed growth and insect attack. The job then is first to establish a healthy lawn by bringing the pH into balance. Your local garden center can assist you in testing and bringing the soil to a pH level between 6.5 and 7.

We can reduce the impact of herbicides and pesticides on our home environment in several ways. First, establish the healthy lawn, to greatly minimize the need for any chemical treatment. Next, we should encourage the natural enemies of insects — birds and other insects — to frequent our yards and gardens.

We should then study the herbicides and pesticides available and use those that are least likely to create future problems. The Ringer Corporation, for example, offers an entire line of pesticides that are not harmful to people, pets, or the environment. And finally, read and follow the application instructions to the letter. Overuse of lawn and garden chemicals through ignoring the application rates is a common source of pollution.

Excess fertilizer and other chemicals will run off the lawn and into nearby lakes or streams, where they encourage the growth of plants that choke off the water, and poison fish and other aquatic wildlife. Apply sparingly, please.

Birds cannot only add color and life to your yard, they also will help to control the insect population. While the woodpecker seems to be attacking your tree, he is actually feeding on insects that could cause the tree harm.

When you water your lawn, robins and other helpful birds spread over the turf, feeding on night crawlers and insects. Martins and swallows feast on mosquitoes. A bird feeder, a bird bath, and a few birdhouses scattered about the place will encourage birds to come and dine. Don't neglect to fill the feeder and bird bath, and bell your cat if you have one.

FARMER/HOMEOWNER USAGES COMPARISON

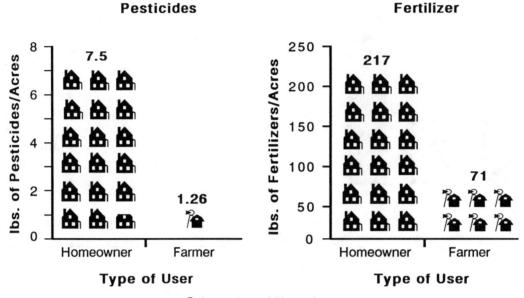

Data courtesy of Ringer Corp.

RELATIVE TOXICITY OF PESTICIDES

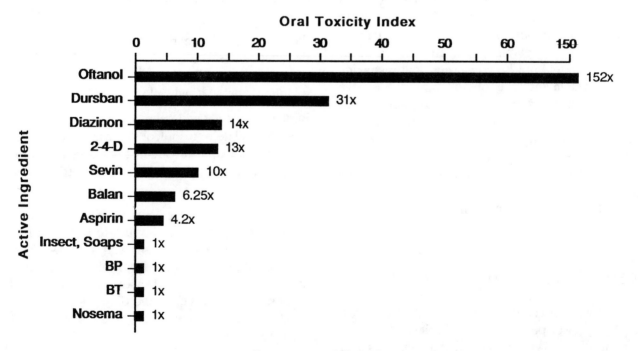

Data courtesy of Ringer Corp.

Pesticides

In trying to eliminate the carpenter ants that burrowed through my timber retaining wall, I spread Diazanon about the place, and sprayed the cracks between the timbers with an aerosol ant killer. The ants grew fat with this treatment, returning in greater size and numbers each spring. Finally, I asked a young man at my home center what product he would recommend for ants. He handed me a can of Ortho's Wasp and Hornet spray. When I sprayed the timbers with this product the ants literally tumbled out of the cracks, dead when they hit the ground. When carpenter bees invaded the siding on my house, I asked a young clerk again what product to use. He suggested the product that I had used for two seasons, without success. The clerk then informed me that I should spray the bees' entry hole *at dusk*, when all the bees had returned to the nest (my house) for the night. Spraying during the day, according to the young man, would avail little.

My point in relating these incidents is that you can pollute the air, spend a lot of money on chemicals, and achieve little success, if you try to choose a product from a shelf and do your own exterminating. So minor a point as the time of application can have very great effect on your success, or lack of same. Shop where there are experts to assist you; study garden guides such as those printed by Ortho to acquaint yourself with the problem and its solution(s) before you race about with spray cans of chemicals and pollute the entire area. And, if you use a pesticide or other product that does not work, take time to write a complaint to the manufacturer. The consumer should not be troubled with chemical products that do not do the job for which they are intended, and you have a right to ask for your money back.

Better yet, seek out non-polluting products that will do the job without fear of exposing the world to dire consequences. Again, the Ringer Corporation makes a series under their "Attack" label. These products are made from extracts of the chrysanthemum flower or from naturally occurring bacteria.

In addition, Ringer offers insecticidal soaps made from potassium salts, useful for fighting mites and aphids, plus traps for both beetles and flying insects. These products can even be sprayed or dusted on vegetables on the day of harvest, without danger to the consumer or to beneficial insects.

Herbicides

The use of herbicides, chemicals for controlling weed growth, can be eliminated from home consumption. Rather, use trimmers such as the Weed Eater, or weed by hand. Use a cultivator or hand tool such as the garden hoe to remove weeds from the garden. Don't cultivate too deeply: about 1 inch deep is enough. This will cut weeds off before they become established. Weed seeds that are turned up in cultivating will be eaten by the birds.

For flower gardens, use plastic weed barriers that prevent weed growth while letting water and air penetrate. These weed barriers can last up to five years.

As mentioned elsewhere in this book, the best herbicide may be mulch. Mulch not only suppresses weed growth, it also helps save water by holding ground moisture. Use mulch in flower or vegetable gardens, or as a decorative touch around trees or shrubbery.

BUILDING A COMPOST BIN

As has been suggested, most households will have neither the need nor the space to build a large compost bin. For those who have the acreage or are ardent gardeners, the need for composting may be much greater than for the average homeowner. Included here are some general guidelines for constructing and maintaining a large compost bin.

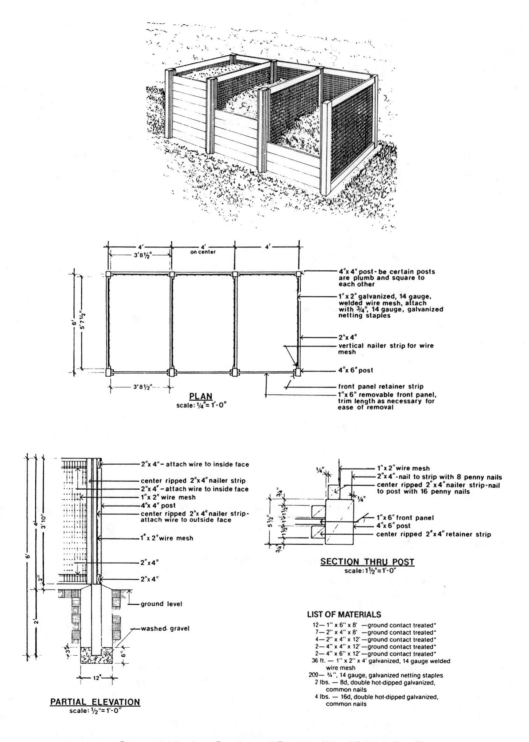

PLAN
scale: ¼" = 1'-0"

4"x 4" post - be certain posts are plumb and square to each other

1" x 2" galvanized, 14 gauge, welded wire mesh, attach with ¾", 14 gauge, galvanized netting staples

2"x 4" vertical nailer strip for wire mesh

4"x 6" post

front panel retainer strip

1"x 6" removable front panel, trim length as necessary for ease of removal

PARTIAL ELEVATION
scale: ½" = 1'-0"

2"x 4" - attach wire to inside face
center ripped 2"x 4" nailer strip
2"x 4" - attach wire to inside face
1"x 2" wire mesh
4"x 4" post
center ripped 2"x 4" nailer strip - attach wire to outside face
1"x 2" wire mesh
2"x 4"
2"x 4"
ground level
washed gravel

SECTION THRU POST
scale: 1½" = 1'-0"

1"x 2" wire mesh
2"x 4" - nail to strip with 8 penny nails
center ripped 2"x 4" nailer strip - nail to post with 16 penny nails
1"x 6" front panel
4"x 6" post
center ripped 2"x 4" retainer strip

LIST OF MATERIALS

12 — 1" x 6" x 8' — ground contact treated*
7 — 2" x 4" x 8' — ground contact treated*
4 — 2" x 4" x 12' — ground contact treated*
2 — 4" x 4" x 12' — ground contact treated*
2 — 4" x 6" x 12' — ground contact treated*
36 ft. — 1" x 2" x 4' galvanized, 14 gauge welded wire mesh
200 — ¾", 14 gauge, galvanized netting staples
2 lbs. — 8d, double hot-dipped galvanized, common nails
4 lbs. — 16d, double hot-dipped galvanized, common nails

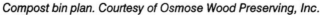

Compost bin plan. Courtesy of Osmose Wood Preserving, Inc.

First, choose your compost site with care. Even a well-maintained compost pile will give off some odors, which may be offensive to nearby neighbors. Build your compost bin(s) so that odors will not be carried to your neighbor's windows.

Next, keep your compost bins within reasonable size limits. As vegetable matter begins to decompose and to give off moisture, it rapidly decreases in volume. Limit the size of the bin to prevent the structure from becoming an eyesore. For the same reason, you will want to plan your construction and choose your building materials with care, so that the finished bins are an attractive project that does not detract from your yard's appearance or from your neighbor's view.

A starting point for planning the dimensions of your compost bin might be a series of two or three joined compartments, each 4 feet high by 4 feet wide by 4 feet long. This would yield a total overall structure size of 4' x 4' x 12' long. For increased capacity, you could make the compost bin wider, but consider limiting the width to what you can comfortably reach across with a shovel or garden fork, because you must be able to turn and tend the materials as they are decomposing. A limit of about 6 feet for the width might be considered the maximum size, with the final decision again depending on how much material you expect to compost.

Select pressure-treated lumber for all the wood components of your composting bin. Be sure the lumber is treated for the maximum limits of wood in contact with the ground. Because the contents of the bin will be constantly wet (you must add moisture as needed to aid decomposition), even the above-ground wood must be ground-contact grade. For the same reasons, i.e., protection in a hostile environment, any wire mesh should be galvanized, and all staples, nails, or screws used in construction should be galvanized, stainless steel, or aluminum to guard against rust and corrosion.

Measure and outline the perimeter of the compost bin on the ground. Check each individual compartment, plus the overall structure outline, to be sure it is square. Use the 3'-4'-5' method, otherwise known as the Pythagorean Theorem, to check that everything is square. The geometric theorem states that, in a right triangle (one with one 90 degree or square angle), the square of the hypotenuse is equal to the sum of the squares of the other two sides. To simplify this theorem, drive a corner stake and run a mason's line from the corner stake to other stakes placed at approximate 90 degree angles from the first stake. Measure out a distance of 3 feet on one side of the mason's line, and measure out 4 feet on the other line, and mark these measurements. Now, move the two lines until the distance between the marks on the two lines is exactly 5 feet, and stake the lines in place. The corner is now square.

Set 4 x 4 posts at the corners of the overall structure, and at the intervals where walls will divide the bins. You should have at least two, or better still, three, separate compartments in the bin. This provision will allow you to have one or two "working" bins, where you are adding vegetation, water, and activator (such as high-nitrogen fertilizer) to begin the breakdown process. As the material in one bin breaks down, you will have compost in various stages of decomposition, from fresh vegetation down to finished humus or compost.

Again, use pressure-treated lumber for the 4 x 4 posts. The posts should be 6 feet long, so they can be set into the ground 2 feet deep, with 4 feet above ground level. Place 3 to 6 inches of gravel in the bottom of the post hole to help drainage and keep water away from the end grain of the post. Set the post in the hole and then fill the post hole with concrete to make it very solid. Use a concrete mix product such as Sakrete for easy concrete mixing.

For the walls of your compost bin, you can use pressure-treated lumber or galvanized wire mesh, or a combination of the two materials. Some prefer to build a treated lumber frame, consisting of 4 x 4 posts and 2 x 4 rails between, then use 1" x 2" x 4' galvanized wire mesh for the side walls and separating partitions between compartments. They then use 1 x 6 pressure-treated lumber for the front gates on the bins. This is an economical alternative to an all-wood bin.

The method for building these front gates for access to the compartments is to nail pressure-treated 1 x 2s to the inside faces of the 4 x 4 corner posts, forming a channel into which one can place the 1 x 6 boards. To gain access to the bin compartments you simply lift out one or more of these 1 x 6 boards from their channels. The 1 x 6 boards are fitted loosely into the channels, not nailed, so one or all of the front gate boards can be removed for access.

Before placing the 4 x 4 posts in the ground, and before assembling other wood components, apply a coat of water repellent such as Thompson's Water Seal or a like product to all sides and edges of the wood, especially to any ends on cut lumber. This water repellent will help the wood resist water attack and should be renewed at least once a year on the above-ground lumber to make the structure last longer. A good practice would be to apply a water repellent to exposed wood each time you clean out the compost from one or more of the bins. The job is easy: spray the water repellent using an ordinary pressure-type garden sprayer.

CHECKLIST
LAWN AND GARDEN

- ❑ Buy and use non-chemical fertilizers, pesticides, and herbicides where available (watch for organic products).

- ❑ Use all garden and yard chemical products sparingly, according to application instructions on the labels. Do not overdose.

- ❑ Buy a mulching mower, or mow more frequently so clippings are shorter (less than 1 inch), so you do not have to bag lawn clippings.

- ❑ Buy or rent a chipper/shredder to break up fall leaves. For small amounts of leaves, place the leaves in a garbage pail and shred them with a weed whacker (string trimmer).

- ❑ Don't collect garden wastes. Instead, leave them on the garden and till them into the soil with a rotary tiller.

- ❑ Turn your garden over in the fall. The tilled soil is loose and holds rain or snow.

- ❑ Have the pH factor of your lawn tested and add nitrogen or sulphur as required to bring your soil into pH balance. A healthy lawn will not need chemicals.

- ❑ Measure the flow of your lawn watering equipment by placing a coffee can, with a 1-inch depth mark painted on it, on the lawn as you water. Time how long it takes for the water in the can to reach the mark, and apply water accordingly. A healthy lawn needs about 1 inch of water per week, including rainfall.

- ❑ Attract birds to your yard to help control garden pests. Put up a bird feeder and bird bath; hang a purple martin house rather than spraying for mosquitoes.

- ❑ Use a garbage disposer to get rid of meat and dairy wastes. Save vegetable scraps, coffee grounds, egg shells for composting; feed bread scraps to birds.

- ❑ Use all vegetable wastes from your yard. If you do accumulate a plastic bag full of waste, pour in a cup of high-nitrogen fertilizer, moisten the waste lightly, and seal the top of the bag. Leave it in sunlight, turn it twice weekly, and you'll have mulch in about thirty days.

- ❑ If you compost, mix perlite (available in garden stores), peat, and compost together to make your own potting soil.

- ❑ Use the coarse cutter on a chipper/shredder to cut twigs and tree limbs into decorative wood chips that can be used for garden paths or ground cover under trees, in flower beds, etc.

- ❑ Have trees professionally trimmed to cut away deadwood and open tree canopies so sunlight can reach grass or roof shingles, as well as to discourage insect infestation.

4
Plastics

Plastics of all types have come heavily under fire as prime polluters. The foam food cartons, rings that hold six-packs of drinks together, plastic bottles, and shrink-wrap food packaging are all indicted as objectionable wastes. Writers on conservation subjects often urge that we choose "less polluting" packaging and leave plastics behind.

With condemnation of plastics in mind, it is fair to ask ourselves a question: given the opportunity to ban plastics from the scene, which products would be banned? Would we ban lightweight automotive parts that have reduced the weight of the cars and thus saved us many millions of barrels of oil? Would we ban packaging with PVC (polyvinyl chloride) plastics that keep food and medical supplies sanitary? How about surgical plastic tubing, bandages, or disposable diapers? Or perhaps we could ban tamper-resistant closures for food and medicine containers, or shatter-resistant bottles that protect us from dangerous accidents. Plastics have been a positive development in many areas of business, not least of which is the protection of fresh foods such as meats, fruits, and vegetables. Perhaps we should take another look at the entire subject of plastics and the pluses and minuses they bring to our lives. If, as with most of new technology, we find that blind abuse of plastic products is the problem, perhaps we can find a middle ground where we reap the benefits while minimizing the polluting consequences of plastics.

PACKAGING

To begin, we have heard that we should reject plastic packaging and choose instead glass or paper/paperboard containers which can be recycled. The plea has several flaws: plastic can be, and is being, recycled. It is true that we are just beginning to recycle plastics, but that objection is true of other packaging as well. Those who urge a return to glass bottles do not consider that glass is heavy, that it costs money to haul it about, that a great deal of energy was once spent on hot water and/or steam to clean and sterilize those bottles. If by recycling you mean to melt the glass object down and reform it into another object, then consider that glass manufacture is highly energy intensive. There is no "free ride" alternative to plastics, because all waste is a result of human activity and all materials have their own unique advantages — and their drawbacks. In point of fact, an estimated 80 percent of waste is presently just dumped in landfills, so recyclability is not the real issue. Further, newspapers or other paper products can be dug out of forty-year-old landfills and still be intact, because modern landfills are managed to *prevent* products from degrading.

A study done in Germany (by the German Society for Research into the Packaging Market, 1987) showed that, if plastic packaging were replaced entirely:

1. The energy used to make packaging would double;

2. The cost of packaging would double;

3. The volume of waste generated would more than double;

4. The weight of packaging would increase four-fold.

If we accept these estimates as correct, we can see that plastics have, among other things, helped to hold down the cost of packaged products, and helped contain the rising cost of living. Shipping costs alone, which are established by weight, would rise dramatically if all those plastic bottles and other products were replaced by glass or some other substitute.

In researching this question I bought a burger and fries from each of three fast-food chains in my neighborhood, to consider the packaging. Each restaurant used similar packaging, so there was little difference in the volume of waste generated from each. A cardboard box for the french fries, a paper or foil wrap for the burger, extra paper napkins, a cash register receipt, and a bag to carry it all in. Is there room for improvement with fast-food packaging? One thing we can rely on is that businesses tend to do what is in their own best interests. That means that you can assume that these huge chains have given much thought to packaging. The fact of the matter is that for the 32 *billion* meals served last year by fast food restaurants, the packaging — paper, plastics, and plastic foam — made up *one-quarter of 1 percent*, by volume or weight, of landfill wastes.

MANUFACTURING

One objection to plastics has been their manufacturing methods. Manufacturers of foam plastics stopped using chlorofluorocarbons (CFCs) in 1988.

One problem with recycling plastics has been that

products that appear to be the same — clear plastic bottles, for example — may be made from different formulas, so they can't be mixed together. Manufacturers of plastics are trying to solve that problem by marking bottles or other products with a code that will indicate the type of plastic used in the manufacture. This will aid in the sorting and recycling of most plastic products.

There are today more than 200 companies in the plastic recycling business. Twenty percent of plastic soft drink bottles (made of polyethylene terephthalate or PET) are being recycled into carpet backing, appliance handles, floor tiles, and auto parts or into fiberfill for pillows, sleeping bags, or ski jackets.

In 1988, 72 million pounds of milk and juice containers (made of high density polyethylene or HDPE) were recycled into traffic cones, non-food bottles, piping, crates, flowerpots, and plastic lumber for decks, boat docks, or park benches.

Polystyrene foam from food trays and containers can be recycled into insulation board, cafeteria food trays, and other home or office products.

Plastics that are of mixed chemistry or "commingled" are recycled to make plastic lumber that becomes traffic barriers, fence posts, and playground equipment.

The final option for plastics, as for other waste materials, is to join the waste stream that fuels the incinerators for a waste/energy conversion. The energy generated by burning these wastes creates steam to drive electricity generators. Once it has been passed through the generators, the steam can be piped to businesses or factories nearby to provide hot water and heating needs.

We are and have been a wasteful society. In the past, as today, the profit motive has driven the business decisions. Plastic offers a low-cost packaging material with no apparent superior substitutes. In the past it has simply been more profitable to throw used containers away than to recycle them. But as more businesses get into plastic recycling, and local communities provide bins for easier sorting and disposal, we may see plastic recycling becoming more common.

USING LESS PLASTIC

As we noted in prior chapters, the most desirable option is "source reduction," or simply consuming less plastic. We have already mentioned in Chapter 3, "Lawn and Garden," that we can eliminate the need for and use of plastic bags now used for leaf and grass disposal. We can accomplish this simply by better management of our lawns and gardens, to return yard waste to the land.

How else to reduce home consumption of plastic? We have the option of using cotton diapers rather than disposable diapers, thus eliminating both the plastic content of the diapers and the human feces from the landfill load. But, as also mentioned, we should not make quick judgments: remember that it takes a great deal of energy to wash and dry diapers and more energy for pickup and delivery if we choose a diaper service. The notion that there are quick and easy solutions to the waste stream problem simply is not true. Keep in mind also that child care centers require disposable diapers, so working parents again are faced with limited options.

Car products such as antifreeze and oil also are packaged in plastic bottles. Home car maintenance may become a less desirable option if we consider that service stations may buy car fluid products in bulk (barrels) and thus eliminate use of plastic bottles. If you consider the problems of disposing of the old oil or other fluids, plus disposing of the used containers, it may be less trouble (although more expensive) to have auto maintenance service work done by the garage.

Plastics Chart

The Society of the Plastics Industry (SPI) has developed a voluntary coding system for plastic containers. This system identifies bottles and other containers by their material type to help recyclers and others in sorting containers. The symbol is designed to be imprinted on the bottom of the plastic container. The numerical code appears inside a three-sided triangular arrow.

HDPE

CODE	MATERIAL	EXAMPLES	MARKETS FOR THE RECYCLED MATERIAL
1	Polyethylene terephthalate (PET)	Soft drink bottles	Skis, surfboards, sailboat hulls, carpeting, fiberfill, paint brushes
2	High-density polyethylene (HDPE)	Milk, water jugs	Drain pipes, boat piers, traffic cones, signs, toys, flower pots, garden furniture, curb stops, portable toolboxes
3	Vinyl	Shampoo bottles	Truck bed inserts, industrial flooring
4	Low-density polyethylene (LDPE)	Ketchup bottles	Mixed plastics: Insulation, office accessories
5	Polypropylene	Squeeze bottles	Park benches, fencing, car stops boat docks
6	Polystyrene	Fast-food packaging	
7	Other		

USES OF PLASTICS IN TODAY'S ECONOMY

Major market shares: 1989

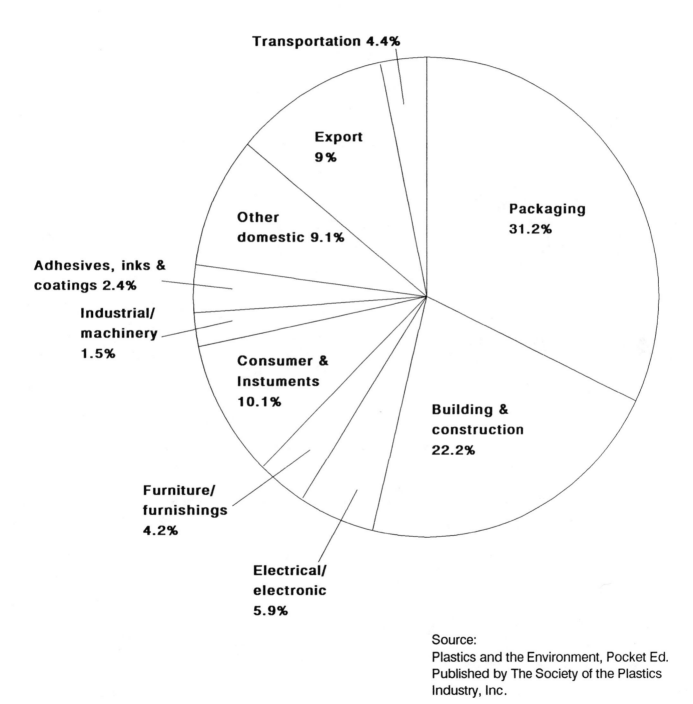

Source:
Plastics and the Environment, Pocket Ed.
Published by The Society of the Plastics
Industry, Inc.

5
Organizing for Home Recycling

Many cities already have persuaded their citizens to cooperate in recycling programs. Estimates are that one-half of all aluminum cans are already being recycled. A suburb near my home estimates that 75 percent of its residents are recycling. Many people who have not joined in the effort have resisted because it appears to be "too much bother." One friend who got the bug early began saving aluminum cans for recycling. The cans were placed in bags, and they soon overwhelmed all the garage space. When he had enough to fill his large station wagon he loaded the cans and hauled them to a recycling center, where he sat in one of the Saturday morning lines. When his turn came, his wagonload of cans netted him about $7.00. End of recycling effort.

If sorting, storing, and hauling household wastes seems too much effort, try to eliminate the hauling step. Many larger cities have waste haulers who have invested in compartmentalized trucks. These trucks have at least four compartments, and will pick up all sorted waste. If your waste collector or city does not accept materials for recycling, check with your local government for advice on the subject. Many youth groups such as churches, athletic teams, and scout organizations pick up recyclables as a fund-raising effort. If entire neighborhoods agree to clean, sort, and stack recyclables by the roadside, salvage companies may agree to pick the waste up on a periodic schedule.

Some cities and waste collection companies offer color-coded or labeled containers to make it easy to sort waste. These containers can be stacked in the garage for future transport to curbside pickup. To avoid frequent trips to the garage you will want to organize for easy waste sorting in your house.

ORGANIZING THE KITCHEN

At the January Home Builders Show in Atlanta were plans for kitchens of the future. Such kitchens may have bins or chutes into which we can sort and store our trash, to make disposal most convenient. If you are building a new house or planning to remodel your present one, by all means consider storage and disposal provisions to make home recycling easy.

Depending on the amount of waste you generate, storage and sorting facilities can be either modest or elaborate. For most small families, a broom closet or pantry can hold wire or plastic baskets for sorting glass, metal containers, papers, and non-recyclables. Companies such as Clairson International, which specializes in kitchen organizers, are busy designing stackable racks, bins, and holders that accept plastic bags. Because most household waste is generated in the kitchen, that is the most likely place for cleaning and sorting waste materials.

Color-coded and stackable recycling bins such as these made by Tucker make it easy to recycle.

This recycling cabinet is the "Double Roll-Out Waste" model from Fieldstone Cabinetry. It fits into an 18-inch wide cabinet space and holds two 16-gallon plastic wastebaskets.

Shop home center or department stores for waste bins that best suit your own family needs. If you are remodeling the kitchen, and you have basement space beneath, consider having modified clothes chutes installed between the wall studs. Unbreakables such as food or beverage cans can be dropped down the chute(s) into plastic containers below. (This is not recommended for homes with young children.)

Ideas for separating, cleaning and storing waste items depend on the item's makeup.

GLASS

Because glass containers are breakable, and the resulting remnants are dangerous, glass requires some time and care for disposal. You should rinse the container, but you need not remove the label(s). Remove any metal rings from twist-off caps. Sort by color: green, amber, and clear glass containers are recyclable. Light bulbs (incandescent or fluorescent) and window glass should be disposed of in the trash, or as directed by your local hauler.

PLASTIC

Plastic beverage containers should be rinsed clean and flattened for storage. Most foam plastic food trays and plastic wraps should be discarded with trash.

PAPER

Keep newsprint separate from magazines and junk mail. An easy way to bundle newspapers is to double them over and insert them into a brown paper grocery bag — you get rid of both at one time.

Paper that has food contact cannot be recycled and must be disposed of as trash. Corrugated cardboard boxes can be flattened (just remove staples, or break the glue bond) and tied into bundles for disposal.

ALUMINUM

Aluminum cans have a high recycle rate because they can be sold for about 1½ cents each. There are twenty-eight aluminum cans in a pound: a pound of cans in my city sells today for 42 cents. Can crushers that can be mounted on the wall or used on a benchtop can be purchased for under $10. These let you flatten the cans for space-saving storage. If you buy beverages by the case (twenty-four cans), and don't care to flatten the cans, put the empty cans back into the box they came in. Wash and save aluminum food trays and other aluminum food containers for recycling.

STEEL CANS

Food cans made of metals other than aluminum should be rinsed to avoid odors and insects. The easiest way to store them is to cut both the top and bottom from the can, place both the top and bottom discs into the cylinder, then flatten the cylinder for storage. The cans won't take up much space this way, and you can store many cans before worrying about disposal.

GARBAGE

Perhaps the easiest and cleanest way to dispose of food wastes is through a sink-mounted garbage disposal unit, rather than burying it in landfills. Whatever method you choose, try to reduce the volume of garbage as much as possible.

Meat and any animal products must be handled as garbage. These products produce offensive odors and attract insects when placed in a compost pile.

A trash compactor can reduce the volume of home trash and aid both storage and disposal. Photo courtesy of Thermador.

But vegetable wastes can be mixed into compost piles rather than being processed into the waste stream. Most vegetable wastes will decompose rapidly and can be mixed with grass or leaves for disposal.

TRASH

Plastic food trays that have held meat, and any plastic or paper wrappers that have had food contact, must go to the landfill or incinerator. If you recycle everything that you possibly can, this segment of your waste should not be large. However, you may want to invest in a trash compactor to reduce trash volume for storage and for pickup.

CHECKLIST

ORGANIZING FOR HOME RECYCLING

☐ Identify a waste hauler (public or private) who takes recyclables in your area and arrange for pickup of your recyclables.

☐ Start a neighborhood cleanup effort.

☐ If you are planning to remodel, consider installing a compartmented disposal bin in the kitchen. Or, if you have a basement beneath the kitchen, consider a chute arrangement.

☐ Research available products for sorting recyclables and buy or build the one most suited to your needs.

☐ Clean and sort glass by color after removing caps and metal rings.

☐ Rinse and sort plastics by type.

☐ Bundle newspapers into brown grocery bags or tie with twine. Sort magazines separately.

☐ Remove and put in the trash any paper materials contaminated by food waste.

☐ Flatten cardboard boxes after removing staples.

☐ Crush aluminum cans if you wish and sell to a scrap metal dealer or recycle. You may wish to rinse cans, especially in summer, to prevent insect infestation.

☐ Rinse steel cans. Flatten for storage if desired.

☐ If remodeling the kitchen, install a garbage disposal.

☐ Start a compost pile for vegetable wastes.

6
Water Conservation

Years ago I read of the musings of a German philosopher, who lamented the role of the Rhine River being used to flush the waste away from German cities. "The Rhine will wash Germany," he said, "but what will wash the Rhine?"

Some 300 miles north of my Minnesota home is a place called Itasca State Park. There a small stream rises; tourists stop there to have their pictures taken, crossing the stream on rocks. The small stream is the headwaters of the Mississippi River.

The Mississippi winds its way southward through Minnesota. Not many miles south of the headwaters is a huge Mississippi Reservoir called Winnibigoshish, one of the great natural walleye fisheries in the world. My best fishing days have been spent on "big Winnie." But even here, in the heart of the Chippewa National Forest, the Department of Natural Resources (DNR) has become concerned about the quality of the water and the advisability of eating fish taken from this water. Some lakes in the area have water problems that have caused the DNR to advise that we eat only one meal of fish per month from these waters.

Further south yet, near my suburban Minneapolis home, is a place called Minnehaha Falls. The park there overlooks the Mississippi and Lock and Dam No. 1. Barge and recreational boat traffic locks through the dam. Nearby, the City of Minneapolis draws its water supply, and a bit farther down dumps its treated sewage back into the river.

As one travels between Minneapolis and the headwaters of the Mississippi, one crosses the meandering river many times. And each time I cross the river I recall the words of my anonymous German philosopher and think: "The Mississippi will wash America, but what will wash the Mississippi?"

Water has become a subject much discussed, both as to quantity and quality, and from sea to sea. We have used our major waterways as sewers, diminishing the quality of the water, of the river and its environs, and of the wildlife that inhabits the river. In the spirit of "clean up your own mess," is it too much to require — to demand — that any city or business that uses the water of a river clean and return the water to the river in as good quality as they found it? Why should citizens pay federal taxes to clean up the mess created by any city or business that chooses to foul our water?

GROUNDWATER

Most of our fresh water is underground, but this water is being contaminated and depleted by careless practices. Abandoned rural wells invite entry of agricultural chemicals. Waste dumps, most of which were established by businesses (but many or most of these businesses were run to make war products for the federal government), continue to foul underground aquifers. The seepage from these chemical dumps will continue as rain water filters through the soil and reaches the aquifers. We are due to reap an unwanted harvest as the early landfills begin to seep their noxious contents to the water tables below.

One report stated that 85 percent of California's water is used for irrigation. The report also stated that one of the major agricultural regions, the San Joaquin Valley, began pumping water for irrigation in 1925. Since that time, the valley floor has sunk 10 feet as the water beneath it was pumped away.

In Minneapolis, many businesses have been permitted to use cold water from underground aquifers for air conditioning. Huge wells are drilled to these underground lakes, and cold water is pumped through air conditioning pipes at tremendous rates. As the water is warmed by ambient temperatures, it is dumped into the Mississippi River. This system, called "once-through" water usage, uses massive amounts of water. A suburban newspaper estimates that 100 Minneapolis businesses, using once-through heating/cooling systems, consume *11 billion gallons* of clean groundwater per year, then dump it into the river.

Groundwater is harmed in two ways: the first is overuse, where we simply pump water faster than it is being replaced. The second problem for groundwater is chemical contamination. These chemicals enter the groundwater from landfills, farms, and other agricultural sources, from city lawns and gardens when rains wash pesticides, herbicides, and fertilizers into lakes or streams.

To deal with this water pollution, we have built or enlarged our sewage treatment plants. But even as we increase treatment capacity we increase water usage, and in times of high sewage volume we see raw sewage being dumped untreated into whatever river or sea is nearby. In addition, storm sewers wash whatever chemicals have been used or spilled upon the land into the river or ocean. Beaches become unusable as everything from waste oil to dumped hospital wastes wash back upon our shores.

One wag has observed that we maintain multiple layers of government so we can pass the blame along. Mayors — even those with billion-dollar budgets — point to governors, who in turn can point to the Congress or the President. Again, mature people think it not unreasonable to expect the person(s) responsible for the mess to clean it up.

REDUCING WATER USE

As individual citizens we cannot do much to affect the global picture. But individuals, collectively, can reduce the use of water by a large degree. The first step is to become aware of what happens when we use water.

Each time we pour water down a drain we are creating sewage. If we drop a tissue into the toilet and flush it, we have created 5 to 7 gallons of sewage. Because all this water flows together, it is all contaminated to the same degree as the most noxious waste. And each flush increases the total number of gallons of sewage that must be treated.

It is estimated that each person in the U.S. uses up to 80 gallons of water per day. It is further estimated that 62 percent, or 50 of those 80 gallons, is wasted. If those numbers fail to impress us, we should consider the many millions of dollars that are spent to build and operate water departments to supply clean water, and sanitary or sewage plants to treat the water we have contaminated. If we would reduce our water usage by 25 percent we could, in a chain reaction, reduce up front the amount of water treated for human consumption, and again after it has been utilized.

Water Usage Per Person, Per Day

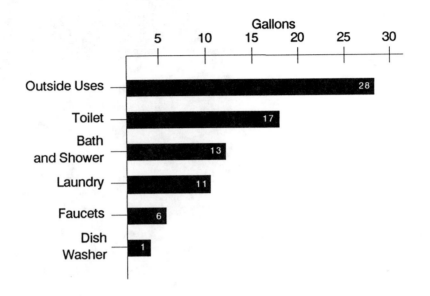

One of our problems is that we have taken our water supply for granted. What is cheaper, or more abundant, than water? As our population and consumption grows, and as we insist on living in arid or desert areas where there is no water, we are bumping up against some very unpleasant facts: the water we drink, the air we breathe, the land that gives us life, all are being made unusable by our flagrant misuse.

Many large cities are now experiencing such water shortages that rationing is becoming a daily fact rather than an emergency measure. What can be done about this waste? Reports state that San Francisco has cut water usage by 25 percent. Conservation measures such as limiting lawn watering and washing cars, have reduced water usage in many other affected cities.

In my own city of Minneapolis, the flow of the Mississippi was so reduced in the summer of '89 that there was talk of drawing down some of the large lakes in northern Minnesota, through which the Mississippi flows, in order to ensure an adequate water supply for Minneapolis. The resort owners, who make their living off tourists and fishermen, were greatly underwhelmed at the idea of dropping their lake levels by 8 inches or more. By summer '90 the rainfall had recovered to the point that there is no water shortage at present. But, apparently, if you have not experienced water rationing, then it is just a matter of time. Water, not oil, may be our next big crisis.

How can the individual act to reduce water pollution and water usage? First, there are new fixtures that let us reduce water consumption. Next, we could manage our lawns better to reduce the amount of water needed for lawn and garden. Finally, we could fix all leaky faucets and fixtures and rid ourselves of wasteful bad habits to eliminate wasted water.

LEAKS

Think for a moment how much water is wasted through leaky supply pipes in antiquated city water

This KWCDOMO shower unit features an infinitely variable control to regulate water flow for water conservation. Photo courtesy of KWC Corp.

systems. Various estimates for the city of New York alone are staggering. We are talking here of water that leaks from underground city water supply pipes. It is estimated that 20 percent of treated water is lost through leaking pipes and mains. Each major city may have to begin a systematic rebuilding of its water system, at least a rebuild of all the water mains, to eliminate leaks as a cause of water shortages.

For the homeowner, consider that our housing stock is growing older, and that the majority of houses are more than twenty-five years old. There are few of these houses that do not have at least one leaky faucet. Each homeowner should check all faucets at laundry tubs, clothes washers, kitchen and bath sinks, and outside faucets to be sure there are no leaks. A leak of one drop per second wastes 2300 gallons of water per year. Now multiply that amount by all the faucets in your home or workplace, and you will see that the potential from leaks alone is enormous. Replace leaky faucets, or repair them, to end waste from leaks.

BAD HABITS

Do you linger under the shower in the morning? Let the water run in the sink while you brush your teeth or wash your hands or hair? Use the toilet as a disposal, and flush the hair from your hairbrush, tissue used to remove makeup, or other trash down the toilet? Do you rinse garden vegetables under running water at the kitchen sink? All of these and more are wasteful habits. Don't throw waste down the toilet: it will not only waste water, but will clog your drains. Shut off the water while you brush your teeth, don't take overlong showers, use flow restrictors on shower heads, rinse garden vegetables in a pail or pan of water and discard the water when it becomes dirty. Don't turn on yard sprinklers and go shopping: place pails that have depth markers painted at 1-inch and 2-inch intervals, and apply only as much water as needed — a total of 2 inches every two weeks, including rain and sprinkling (see Lawn section).

If you wash your car at home, rinse the car to remove grit or dirt, wash the car with a pail and sponge, then use the hose to rinse the soap off the washed car. Leaving the hose running while you wash the car can waste a lot of water. Consider running your car through an automated wash rather than washing it at home. The automated equipment may be more efficient than washing the car with a hose.

Save water generated by your dehumidifier and/or air conditioner. Don't pour the water down the drain. Such water is free of minerals and can be used when you change your radiator antifreeze (the mineral-free water is better for your radiator), in steam irons, or poured on houseplants or gardens. Poured down the drain, this clean water becomes so much sewage, sewage that has to be treated before it is dumped into the river.

PLUMBING FIXTURES

The largest water usage from fixtures is from the toilet, which uses an estimated 5 billion gallons per day, wasting 3½ billion gallons. Next comes bathing and showers, laundry, dishwashing, and then the miscellaneous activities such as cooking and cleaning. Most of the fixtures can be easily replaced to cut water usage. At least, when you are ready to remodel the kitchen, bath, or laundry, shop for the most water-conserving fixtures you can find.

Shower Heads

Old-style shower heads have a water flow of 5 to 8 gallons per minute, wasting 1½ billion gallons of water daily. By contrast, the Massage 8 by Teledyne uses 3 gallons of water per minute. Thus we could save at least 10 gallons of water per three-minute shower: four people showering per day = 40 gallons of water saved each day, or almost 15,000 gallons saved per year for a family of four. Don't forget, too, that when the water you save is hot water, you are also saving the energy to heat the water. Remember that three minutes is a long time in the shower, and was a time used as an example, not as a recommendation.

Toilets

The worst offender for wasting water is the toilet. We have seen estimates of eight flushes per day, average, for a home toilet. We think that estimate is low, but for the moment we will accept it as true.

Old-style toilets use 5 to 7 gallons per flush. Modern units available will flush using only 3 to 3½ gallons, for a savings of 2 to 4 gallons per flush. But true water-savers can be flushed with only 1½ gallons of water, saving 3 to 5 gallons per flush. A savings of 3 gallons per flush x 8 flushes per day = 24 gallons of water saved per day. If we multiply 365 days x 24 gallons = 8,760 gallons saved annually.

If you can't afford to replace the toilet just now, you can install water-saving devices in the old water closet. The least expensive step is just to adjust the float level screw, or bend the float rod down. Or place a plastic gallon jug filled with water in the water closet, to displace one gallon. This could save the average family between 3,000 and 5,000 gallons of water per year. Displacing 1 gallon of water will reduce water used by 1 gallon per flush, without affecting the toilet operation.

One device, called the Mini-Flush Water Saver, can save between 2 and 5 gallons of water per flush, depending on the size of your particular water tank. This device has two parts. A float rides at water level in the tank, just as most flush mechanisms do. But the second part is an actuator that is installed over the flow pipe. When the toilet is flushed this device closes the flapper valve so less water is let through. The device costs about $15, and is available through Mini-Flush Co., Inc., Yorba Linda, CA (800) 969-0693.

Keep in mind that total annual savings here are based on an estimated flush frequency of eight times per day. We would estimate that, for a family, you should calculate your own potential savings on a basis of four flushes per day, per person, or six-teen flushes per day total, for a family of four. The water saved by each example would then be double the estimates based on eight flushes per day.

If you install a low-flush toilet, keep in mind that any toilet manufacturer recommends that the only paper you flush down the toilet is toilet tissue. Package wrappings and other papers may clog a low-flow toilet drain.

Laundry

To conserve water in the laundry, wash only full loads and select your cycle carefully. Using the permanent press cycle can mean an extra rinse, which can mean an extra water fill. You can save hot water if you use cold-water detergents and run on the cold temperature setting only.

Dishwashing

How much water would you use by hand-washing your dishes? Hand washing can use 5 gallons of water per minute, if you let water run constantly as you wash and rinse. By contrast, a light wash in a dishwasher will save 8 to 10 gallons of water. Again, as with laundry, you'll save water if you only run the dishwasher when it is full. Open the door after washing and let the dishes air dry to save the energy from the drying cycle.

Try to position your water heater as close as possible to the kitchen and bath, to avoid long pipe runs. A lot of water is wasted just by running all the cold water from the hot water pipe down the drain, waiting for the water to get hot at the faucet. If you can't move your water heater, at least insulate your hot water pipes.

If you don't have a dishwasher, use the plug in the sink and run the sink full of hot water. Wash the dishes in the sink, then set them to drip in a dish rack. When you have finished the dishes, rinse the soap away using the sink's spray nozzle. Don't leave the rinse water running.

A BETTER LAWN WITH LESS WATER

As we stated in Chapter 3 on "Lawns," a lawn that is properly prepared will use fewer chemicals such as pesticides, fertilizers, and herbicides. But there are steps that will also save water while improving lawn health and quality. Some of these points overlap, but they are worth repeating.

The first step for all-round conservation is to get the lawn in good shape. In order for your lawn to use nutrients, you must establish and maintain the right pH balance (pH stands for "potential hydro-gen"). Most lawn experts recommend a neutral pH of between 5 and 7, which means the soil is neither acid nor alkaline. A low pH means the soil is acid, and you must add lime to increase the pH factor. Your local garden center can calculate the amount of lime necessary to bring the pH into balance. A high pH (most common in southern states) indicates that the soil is alkaline, and you may add sulphur to lower the pH and bring it into the neutral range. You will see that your lawn needs fewer chemicals and less water for good main-tenance when pH is brought into neutral range.

Check your soil for compaction. Soil that is too dense can be aerated with a machine that punches holes in the turf. These finger-size holes let air and water penetrate to the roots. You can also top-dress the lawn with topsoil (black dirt) or peat moss to loosen soil. In areas of heavy clay, a layer of sand can be spread atop the turf and tilled in if you decide to do a complete lawn renovation.

Natural lawn fertilizers can improve soil quality by adding bone meal, feather meal, and soya. Products such as Ringer's Lawn Restore also add microorganisms, which reduce compaction and therefore the amount of water needed.

Thatch once was thought to be caused by grass clippings. According to the John Deere spokesman, thatch is most often the result of too-light watering. The grass roots come to the lawn surface seeking water and nutrients, rather than going deep, and these surface roots cause thatch. A lawn made bumpy by night crawlers (large worms) is a sure indication of thatch. You can reduce the population of night crawlers by using a chemical called Diazanon, but the non-chemical solution is to simply de-thatch the lawn. You can rent a de-thatching machine, or buy a dethatching attachment for your lawn mower.

Thatch buildup means your lawn will need more water and will be more easily damaged by drought, so that removal is essential to good lawn health. Remove thatch when it is ½" deep or more.

Drought-Resistant Grass Seed

Because the grass never gets long enough to "seed out" or reseed itself, you must reseed the lawn periodically. For bare spots, or spots where the grass has worn thin, use drought-resistant lawn seeding for reseeding. Drought resistant grasses have deep root systems, so they can draw water from subsurface depths. Grasses such as tall fescues, zoysia grass, Bermuda grass, and St. Augustine grass are all examples of drought-resistant grasses that need less moisture. Ask your local lawn dealer to recommend a grass variety that will grow well in your climate.

Chemical Use

Agriculture is the chief culprit in the use of fertilizers, herbicides, and pesticides. But on a per-acre basis the average homeowner uses *ten times* as much of these chemicals as farmers do. Search out non-polluting, natural lawn aids. Read and follow label directions, and apply all chemicals at or below the recommended spread rate.

Apply nitrogen at a rate that will permit your lawn to grow continuously but slowly. Excess nitrogen may wash off the lawn and pollute lakes or rivers, and it will force grass production, so you have just that much more grass to dispose of or deal with. Two to four pounds of nitrogen per 1,000 square feet of lawn per year will suffice for a healthy lawn.

In addition to quantity, timing is important for good fertilizer application. Proper timing ensures that any fertilizer added will yield a maximum benefit for your lawn. The rule for proper timing is to apply the first fertilizer treatment in the spring, after the grass has started to turn green, and again in late fall. It is best to check with your own lawn dealer for advice on when to apply fertilizer.

You should also find that, having brought your lawn up to proper pH balance, it will require less fertilizer to keep it green and growing. Lawn clippings left to return nutrients to the soil can often replace one fertilizer treatment per year.

Cutting the Grass

Scalping the lawn, or cutting it down to ground level to reduce the number of mowings needed, can let sun and wind dry out grass roots, evaporate precious moisture, and can also encourage attacks from weeds and pests. Let the grass grow long, especially during the heat of the summer.

Grass should be allowed to grow to a height of 3 inches, then clipped back to 2-inch height, never cutting away more than one-third the grass leaf at

A water-saving toilet need not be purely functional. This Alouette Lite™ model has an 18th century French floral design and uses only 1.5 gallons of water per flush. Photo courtesy of Kohler Co.

This water-saving toilet is the Aqualine by Eljer. It uses only 1.5 gallons of water per flush. Photo courtesy of Eljer, Inc.

This kitchen faucet design offers a retractable water wand with a retractable spray head, anti-scald adjusters, and an infinitely variable control for water conservation. Photo courtesy of KWC Corp.

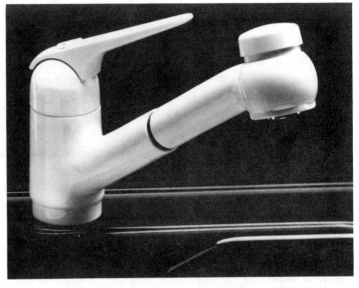

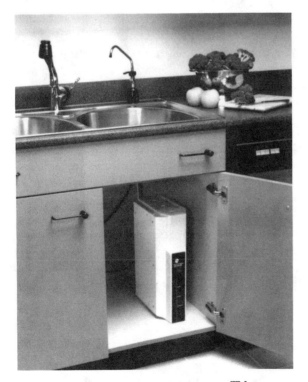

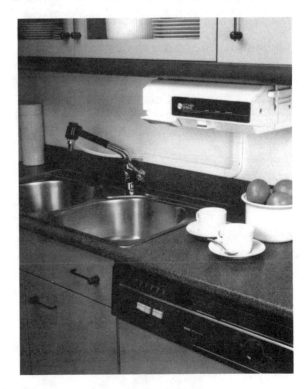

Drinking Water System™ is a water purifier that can be mounted under the sink or under top cabinets and produces up to 25 gallons of clean drinking water daily. Photos courtesy of Kitchen Spring™.

one cutting. Cutting too much leaf at once can make the grass more susceptible to stress and drought. The tall grass will shade the turf from direct sunlight and will retain moisture, while discouraging weed growth by crowding out weeds. Remember also that tall grass means deep roots. Roots that reach deep for subsurface moisture help make the grass more drought-resistant.

Watering the Lawn

Two inches of water, applied every two weeks, will keep the lawn healthy. Count the amount of rainfall you have had in the past two weeks, and subtract the rainfall depth from the 2-inch total. Measure 1 inch and 2 inches up from the bottom of coffee cans, and paint a mark at the 1-inch and 2-inch depths. Then set the coffee cans on the lawn while the sprinklers are running. Check the amount of water in each can, and don't move the sprinklers until that area has received the required amount of water: 2 inches, minus recent rainfall. Then move the sprinklers to the next area, being sure that the areas being watered overlap for complete coverage.

When you have finished watering the lawn, wait twelve hours. Then push a screwdriver into the turf: if it penetrates easily to a depth of 5 or 6 inches, the deep watering is complete.

Although most experts do not recommend light watering, some experts state that a quick shower — called "syringing" — of the lawn surface can cool the grass and help preserve it. Do this at sundown on the hottest days.

Mulching

Mulching and ground covers can moderate soil temperatures, reduce weed growth, and conserve water. Cover areas under trees and shrubs with a mulch. You can recycle yard waste such as tree limbs from pruning or storm damage. Just run the limbs through a shredder (rented or owned).

Ground covers are also available at lawn centers. You can use cedar chips, bark from redwood trees, peat moss, or even decorative stone, depending on the application. Decorative stone will prevent soil erosion, and inhibit weed growth. If you lay a sheet of polyethylene plastic on the ground, making cutouts for flowers, rose bushes, or shrubs, you can then place the decorative stone on top of the plastic. The plastic sheeting also reduces moisture loss, because moisture cannot evaporate upward through the plastic.

As this is being written, experiments continue to develop grasses that require less water and grow more slowly. These grasses of the future will need little water, and very little maintenance or mowing. Already available are chemicals that can impede and slow grass growth. But most thoughtful recyclers will have a bit of trouble trying to justify the addition of yet more types of chemicals into the environment. Our premise is that we can get by without many of the chemicals we now use, not that we want to introduce more.

CHECKLIST

WATER CONSERVATION

❑ Wash the car with a sponge and pail to use only 15 gallons of water, vs. running the hose, which uses up to 150 gallons of water.

❑ Install a low-flow toilet and save up to 5 gallons per flush. Place a plastic gallon milk jug of water in the toilet tank to save 1 gallon of water with every flush.

❑ Fix all plumbing leaks. A leaking toilet can account for 5 percent of water used.

❑ Use water-saving shower heads to cut water usage in half: from 35 gallons per five minute shower to 17 gallons per five minute shower.

❑ Turn off the faucet while brushing teeth to reduce water usage from 5 gallons to ½ gallon.

❑ Turn off faucet while washing dishes to cut water usage from 30 gallons to 5 gallons.

❑ Turn off faucet while shaving and cut water usage from 15 gallons to 1 gallon.

❑ Have your water tested for quality before buying in-home water treatment devices, or ask your city for water test results. For more information on drinking water call the EPA at (800) 426-4791.

❑ Don't buy distilled water. Catch and save water from your dehumidifier or air conditioner rather than letting it run down the drain. Use this water in steam irons, for filling car radiators, to water house plants, or in the garden.

❑ If you have a wet basement, ground water seeping into the basement is running down floor sewer drains and being converted to sewage. Attack basement water problems from the *outside*: install or repair roof rain gutters, correct the grade of your lawn so it slopes away from the basement.

❑ Don't over-water lawns. Let grass grow to 2 inches high to reduce watering needs; apply 1 inch of water per week, including rainfall, to avoid wasting water. The best watering choice is an automatic sprinkling system that is automatically metered.

7
Cars

Suppose we all bought Mercedes cars, maintained them with great care, and extracted 1,200,000 miles of driving from them? At least one driver has done that: that car holds the Guinness World Record for the most mileage ever from any car. Or suppose we each bought a DeLorean with all-stainless steel body, a car with a body that would virtually last forever? Or perhaps we all drive Audis, with galvanized bodies and layers of protective finishes. Would we produce less automotive waste and reduce pollution? Of course we would: in conservation as in economics the principle is still the same — quality does not cost, it pays. And if that is true of the entire car, it is equally true of all its many parts. By buying quality we can practice source reduction, reducing the waste stream by consuming less.

If you read *Consumer Reports* magazine, you know that one important rating of new and used cars is frequency of repairs. This is a valuable guide because it reduces your cost of ownership, plus reducing your car's contribution to the waste stream. This, plus a consideration of the average mileage of the vehicle in question, should play a very important role in helping you decide which car to buy.

But no matter how durable your car is, it will use 4 or 5 quarts of oil for each 3,000 miles you travel. Antifreeze must be replaced about every 20,000 miles; gasoline flows through the car at the rate of 15 to 30 miles per gallon, batteries wear out and

present a disposal problem, and tires may be the most difficult disposal problem of all. It will pay us to give some serious thought to the question of replacement parts for our cars.

ENGINE TUNEUPS

Americans are notoriously lax about regular car maintenance. When I was Senior Editor at the *Family Handyman* magazine we began a regular column called "Handyman Garage," and asked Bobby Unser to contribute to the column. Unser, a top race driver, opined that any American car should last for at least 150,000 miles, if drivers would only do one thing: replace the car's fluids at regular intervals, per the owner's manual specifications. The critical fluids are, of course, oil, antifreeze, and transmission fluid. Replacing the fluids also means replacing the various filters to keep the fluids clean.

The term "tuneups" is still used, but modern cars do not need the same sort of tuneup that was done when cars had distributors. Instead, the term tuneup refers to replacing air filters, cleaning fuel injectors, and replacing spark plugs and plug wires.

Dirty air filters can reduce the flow of clean air for combustion. Modern injectors usually mix air with fuel in a 15:1 ratio. If the air filter is dirty, that ratio can drop to 10:1 or even 7:1 air-to-fuel mix.

Replace your air filter according to the instructions in your owner's manual. Many people think dust or dirt alone is the culprit in plugging air filters, but experts point out that chemicals used for snow removal can also plug filters in winter.

Fuel injectors can be finicky, and you must choose your gasoline with care. Some gasolines contain detergents that keep cleaning injectors as you drive. The best idea is to choose a fuel that has multiple detergents. *Consumer Reports*, in a comparison of fuels, pointed out that Audi, the German car make, recommended only Amoco for their cars, because Amoco had four detergents. The article stated that other gasoline makers such as Phillips 66 were planning to increase the number of detergents in their gasoline as of early 1990. Check with your own dealer to be sure you are getting detergent protection at all temperatures and in all situations.

When you buy gasoline at a self-service station you should set the shut-off on the nozzle. When the nozzle shuts down, do not engage the fuel lever to "top off" the fuel tank, because spilled gasoline can react in sunlight to release volatile organic compounds or VOCs. VOCs cause ground level ozone or smog. You can also buy fuel additives that clean injectors, but choose these with care. You will be better off — and money ahead — to use premium fuels that burn cleaner than to add cleaners at a price of three to five dollars per tankful.

Remember that good maintenance can add up to 10 percent to your mileage figures. This means you can, in effect, reduce the price of gasoline by 10 percent and reduce your annual fuel consumption by that amount. Less fuel consumed means less pollution.

Organizing your daily schedule can also reduce your fuel consumption. Prepare your bills and correspondence for mailing when you are out shopping, and do your shopping on the trip home from work, to minimize those needless trips. Better yet, car pool to work, take turns driving with a relative or neighbor when shopping, keep tires inflated, and observe speed limits. I saw recent estimates that we could save 200,000 barrels of oil *per day* if we would just do these three things (car pool, observe speed limits, and inflate tires properly). Add these savings to the 10 percent savings from proper maintenance mentioned above, and you begin to realize the possible scope of the savings, and the resultant reduction in pollution. And remember, using cruise control whenever possible will make the engine run more efficiently and increase gasoline mileage.

One final point is in order. Although premium gasoline may contain extra detergents for cleaning fuel injectors, the primary purpose for high octane gasoline is to reduce "pinging" or pre-ignition of the fuel in the cylinders. Some auto experts recommend that you burn a tankful of premium or high octane fuel occasionally, for the added detergent benefits, to keep fuel injectors clean.

Keep in mind, however, that it requires more crude oil to make a gallon of high octane premium gas than to make a gallon of unleaded or regular gas, hence the higher pump price for premium fuel. Gasoline industry experts point out that, at the time of the Iraqi invasion of Kuwait, U.S. motorists were choosing premium gasoline about half of the time, even though most or many of their cars were intended to run on 87 octane unleaded. This practice is wasteful and is due to a misconception about the values of premum gasoline.

It is not true that your car will get better mileage using premium; fuel consumption is unaffected by raising the octane. The higher octane simply prevents an engine from "pinging." So, if your engine does not "ping" when using 87 octane gas, you are wasting your money using the higher-priced product. If you doubt this, set the trip meter in your car and check a tankful of unleaded 87 octane gas against a tankful of premium gas of 91 octane, for miles per gallon. You will find no difference, except for the cost.

Keep a close check under the car hood. Replace oil, air, and gas filters at the intervals suggested in your owner's manual, and use a quality oil to extend the life of your car and avoid repairs.

OIL

Remember the good old days, when the oil companies were buying full-page ads in the newspapers, to plead their case for continuing tax breaks via "oil depletion allowances"? In those years 1969-70 their plea was that they provided the nation with a "plentiful supply of cheap oil," so they deserved a tax break.

Today, as Iraq is willing to go to war to hold onto the oil riches of Kuwait, oil accounts for about one-third of our trade deficit, something on the order of $40 billion a year. While we picket industry for their evil polluting ways, industry contributes 20 percent of the air pollution, and our cars contribute 60 percent.

Or consider the oil spill by the *Exxon Valdez*. We picketed Exxon stations and accused them of being poor corporate citizens. Meanwhile, do-it-yourself car owners dumped 400 million gallons of used oil in the trash, down drains, or onto the soil — an amount equal to *thirty-five* tanker accidents *per year*. If you doubt that the *Exxon Valdez* spill was small potatoes compared to our daily spoilage,

drive the nation's highways and check the black streak down the center of each lane. That streak is from the oil and antifreeze that leaks from the underside of our cars. We don't even fight engine and transmission leaks to conserve oil and stop pollution.

Our first step in reducing pollution from oil is to tighten all the bolts where oil or transmission fluid could leak. Next, used oil can be remanufactured to new oil specifications, according to the EPA. Any business that sells motor oil must accept used oil for recycling, or post a sign to direct customers to a nearby disposal center. Transmission fluid, gear oil, and brake fluid can be disposed of with motor oil.

Some car manuals recommend that you change motor oil every 6,000 to 7,000 miles, or twice annually, whichever comes first. Most auto mechanics (and oil dealers) recommend more frequent oil replacement. What should we do? First, understand that oil does not "wear out": it gets dirty and it becomes diluted during the combustion process. There is a fortune waiting for the man who can devise a better oil filter, to keep oil cleaner for more miles. Until that happy day, it may be a better move for the environment — and certainly for your pocketbook — to err on the conservative side. Buy the best filters you can find, and change oil at 3,000 to 4,000 miles, or whenever it looks dirty. Better to waste a little oil than to destroy an engine.

Oil additives are not recommended by most oil companies. All those products that promise to make oil more slippery, stop leaking, and reduce ring blow-by are generally considered to be a waste of money, and an unneeded contribution to the problem of waste disposal. Use a quality oil, without additives.

ANTIFREEZE

Antifreeze is a poisonous chemical, namely ethylene glycol, and should not be mixed in with oil for disposal. You can extend the life of your radiator and engine by keeping fresh antifreeze in your car in a 50/50 mix of antifreeze and water.

To dispose of antifreeze, you can drop it at chemical waste deposit sites run by your local government. If your house is served by a municipal sewer system, you can pour used antifreeze down the sewer drain, and the sewer treatment plant will process it with other sewer wastes. This advice is for homeowners only — those who have limited amounts of antifreeze for disposal. Auto service centers should check with local codes for disposing of large amounts of the fluid.

When using or handling antifreeze, keep in mind that it has a slightly sweet taste that may be attractive to young children and pets. Check and stop any leaks in your radiator or hoses as soon as you see greenish-yellow or red puddles on the driveway, and keep the fluid away from pets and children. Don't dump antifreeze down septic systems. The antifreeze will kill bacteria that are needed by the septic tank to break down wastes. Septic tank

owners should dispose of antifreeze with other hazardous chemicals, at waste sites approved or operated by local governments.

BATTERIES

Car batteries contain about 18 pounds of lead, plus acids, and are very toxic to the environment if improperly disposed of. The good news is that batteries can be remanufactured, so the lead is continually recycled rather than being discarded.

The recommended disposal for used car batteries is to trade them in at replacement time. Battery sales outlets will charge you $5 if you don't bring your old battery in for recycling, but will refund the money when you bring in the old battery. The dealers send the old batteries to shops that remanufacture them.

One way for the consumer to reduce the number of batteries in the waste flow is to buy long-life batteries that are guaranteed for sixty months (five years) or more. If you are buying a new car you may be able to specify a "heavy-duty battery" as an inexpensive option. The heavy-duty batteries often cost only a few dollars more than light-duty batteries that will provide only three or four years of service and will thus increase the volume of batteries in the waste stream.

TIRES

In the Midwest we have seen a steady increase in the number of fires reported at tire disposal sites. One recent fire in Minnesota involved the burning of more than 300,000 tires. And small wonder: there is a total of 2.5 to 3 billion tires in the discard piles, and 280 million more tires are discarded each year.

Discarded tires are piled in unsightly heaps, give off toxic smoke when burned, and are difficult to

Check tire air pressure weekly. Inflate tires to the maximum pressure as indicated on the sidewall of the tire. Have all tires balanced and keep the front end aligned for best tire wear and gas mileage.

dispose of. A landfill operator one day demonstrated for me the difficulty of burying old tires. As he pushed against the mountain of tires with his bulldozer, the tires compressed, then flew from the pile like so many 2-foot Frisbees. If buried or abandoned, the tires last forever with little decomposition. They are such a disposal problem that a tire recycler in northern Minnesota claimed that he could get all the free tires he wanted, trucked in from 600 miles away (Chicago), just by supplying a place where dealers might rid themselves of them. Used tires are harder to throw away than a used boomerang, yet they offer what could be a valuable resource.

Each used tire contains the energy equivalent of 2 gallons of oil. They burn with fearsome heat: the energy value of rubber, per pound, exceeds the energy value of coal. Oxford Energy Corporation, at an electricity generating plant in Modesto, CA, burns five million tires annually and produces enough electricity in the process to power 1,500 houses.

Another disposal option is to remanufacture or retread the tires. If the tires are turned in while the

carcass is still sound, new tread can be formed onto the carcass, and the tire's life is extended. As late as the 1960s, tires were being reclaimed at more than thirty factories in the U.S. Today, tire construction has become more complicated, and economic factors have reduced — almost ended — tire reclamation. It is simply cheaper just to throw the old tires away, but as one spokesman has pointed out, there is no longer any "away." There are simply fewer places to dump used tires.

For the consumer interested in reducing the waste problem, several options exist. Through improved construction and better tire chemistry the life of tires has been greatly extended. Tires that would last for 30, 40, or 50,000 miles were unheard of when I began driving in the early '50s. In my father's day, tires lasted perhaps 2,000 miles, because they had cotton fibers rather than steel or fiberglass belts. Moisture entered through cracks in the rubber and rotted the cotton fibers. When nylon fibers were available, it was a great advance in tire life, and steel belts have again extended our mileage expectations.

But by our carelessness we reduce the life of the

tire and add to the disposal glut. Tire manufacturers will tell you with some exasperation that people simply will not maintain the proper air pressure in their tires. A tire that is not properly inflated rolls with greater friction, increases tread wear, uses more gasoline, and wears out quickly. We could greatly extend tire life if we would carry a tire pressure gauge in our cars, and check tire pressure weekly, or at least monthly.

Another way to extend tire wear is to have tires rotated at the manufacturer's recommended intervals. The theory here is that rotating the tires — moving the tires from front to back, or crisscrossing them from corner to corner — will even out tire wear, so that one or two tires do not wear out prematurely. This tire rotation will usually be done at little cost by your dealer. Do you do it? If so, you belong to a very small club.

Another tire maintenance step is to have tires balanced and aligned. In balancing the tires, lead weights are added around the wheel rim to compensate for any uneven weight distribution of the tire. The tire will roll more smoothly, with less bumping and thumping, if it is balanced. Driving pleasure is increased, and tire wear is extended if tires are balanced. This option is usually offered at a price of $2-3 per tire when you buy new tires.

The front tires of a car sit on pivots that permit the tires to be turned and the car steered. Because the tires will spread slightly as they roll and gain speed, the tire at rest sits rather pigeon-toed, with the wheels and tires turned slightly inward. This is called "toe-in." The tire also can be adjusted from top to bottom, so the tire is hitting the pavement evenly without excessive wear. This is called the "caster and camber" of a wheel.

The attitude of the tire can greatly affect tire wear. A tire that is out of alignment does not roll straight down the highway; rather it is pushed sideways as it rolls. The extra wear on the tire is obvious. Have your car's front end aligned when the car is new (I know you should not have to

worry about this with a new car, but you do — many cars have poor alignment from the factory). Then, as you drive, be alert to any wiggling or vibration that you feel in the steering wheel. This vibration often will not be apparent at low speeds, so if you drive only in the city you may not notice it. It is important to have the alignment checked on the new car, and at periodic service checks afterwards. It is especially important to check alignment after hitting a curb or pothole, where one or more wheels got a hard bounce. Proper alignment and inflation can greatly extend the life of your tires and reduce tire waste streams.

Tire prices are based on tire quality, and tires with wear warranties of 50,000 miles or more cost more than budget tires that offer 30,000 mile warranties. Obviously, the low-budget tire will add as much waste per unit as the quality tire, so we would discourage buying the cheaper tires. If you check ads for tire sales, you will see that each time you gain another 10,000 miles of wear on the tire warranty, you will pay about $10 more for the tire. The quality tires are the bigger bargain, doubly so if you drive a lot of miles per year. Remember, too, that the only contact your car has with the highway is through those four tires, each of which has a highway contact area about the size of your foot. This small contact area is what keeps your car on the road, provides traction in problem driving such as wet or icy highways, and also provides the sole stopping surface in an emergency. Quality tires are important to your safety and the safety of others, so buy good tires and maintain them properly.

To avoid road problems with tires, have the mechanic check them when the car is on the lift for any reason. If the mechanic is under the car, he can easily check the tires for cuts, uneven tire wear, and nails or other objects that may have penetrated through the tire body and will soon cause a flat tire. Checking tire condition can save you a walk home or an expensive towing fee.

Many companies are experimenting with finding

uses for reprocessed rubber. The tires can be shredded and the rubber can be ground as fine as talcum powder. The powder can be mixed with various chemicals and cooked in vats called digesters to make a polymer that can be molded into many products. Experimental products made from recycled rubber include liners for pickup truck beds, waste bins, and surface materials for roads.

A company called Rubber Asphalt Producers Group, headquartered in Phoenix, Arizona, suggests topping roads with rubber-based asphalt. They claim that although the rubber-base product costs about 40 percent more than the usual asphalt material, it can last up to three times as long. Six million tires — 45,000 tons of rubber — were used in roads last year. Estimates are that if 25 percent of paving was rubber we could recycle as many as 200 million tires per year. The U.S. generates about 250 million worn-out tires per year, or about one for each U.S. citizen.

BUY TROUBLE-FREE CARS

As we mentioned at the beginning of the chapter, one key to reducing pollution is to buy those cars that have proven to be most trouble-free. Various car magazines rate cars via "Editor's Tests": *Consumer Reports* compares new cars and issues annual reports on the frequency of repairs of various makes and models. One car survey that is closely watched by the auto industry is conducted by J.D. Power and Associates. Although some of the winners in the Power surveys are obviously among the pricier cars to buy, at least half the winners are mid-priced cars that are within the budget of most of us.

Aside from frequency of repairs, the least polluting cars are obviously those that get the best gas mileage. One cautionary note is in order in this area, however: in accidents, small cars almost always lose to big cars. One auto body mechanic I know uses the comparison of bricks and eggs:

which one wins if you hit them together? With this in mind, it is poor policy to buy a car on the basis of mileage alone. The single most important item to consider when buying a car is crashworthiness. Buy something with enough structure to enable you to survive a crash. It is small solace to know that although you didn't survive the crash, you were getting 30 miles per gallon at the time of the accident.

An odd recent development in the car business was the rise in popularity of 4-wheel-drive sport vehicles among the yuppies, at the very time when concern for the environment was supposedly at its height. Such vehicles are not noted for their conservative ways: gas mileage is generally lower on 4-wheel-drive cars and trucks. There are few sights more ridiculous than a 4-wheel-drive rig with a Greenpeace bumper sticker. If you don't own a ranch, but do drive a 4-wheeler, you don't understand the problem.

1990 Winners

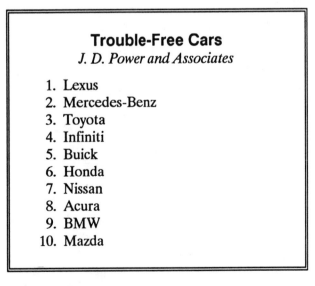

Trouble-Free Cars
J. D. Power and Associates

1. Lexus
2. Mercedes-Benz
3. Toyota
4. Infiniti
5. Buick
6. Honda
7. Nissan
8. Acura
9. BMW
10. Mazda

SAVING GAS

During the oil crisis of the '70s we assembled a list

of tips to save gas. Some we have mentioned in earlier copy, but we believe they bear repeating.

- When buying a new car, check fuel efficiency stickers; check frequency of repair in automotive magazines. Do not surrender crashworthiness for gas mileage, however.

- Reduce speed. Driving at 70 mph requires as much as 20 percent more fuel than driving at 55 mph.

- Use your cruise control whenever traffic permits. Cruise control uses fuel most efficiently.

- Take heavy objects out of the car, but keep luggage inside the car when traveling. Rooftop carriers create wind resistance and cut mileage.

- To gain 4 to 8 percent in mileage, keep the car tuned.

- During hot weather use the air conditioning when driving at high speeds. Open windows create air resistance and cost fuel.

- Maintain proper air pressure in tires. Tires that are underinflated by 5 pounds cut fuel economy as much as 10 percent.

- When waiting for traffic or for a passenger, shut off the engine if the wait will be more than one minute. An engine running at idle will use ½ gallon of gas per hour.

- Don't buy fuel additives that promise better fuel mileage. None has been proven to work.

CAR REPAIRS

In the past, auto salvage yards have been criticized for their sometimes lax housekeeping habits. You've seen the salvage or wreckage yards where hundreds of elderly or wrecked hulks are strewn about. In some communities the salvage yards have been ordered to build fences or otherwise conceal their messy premises from view, but the truth is that these salvage yards serve a vital purpose in recycling used auto parts.

Most professional mechanics will not install used auto parts, for at least two reasons. First, they do not want to be responsible for the future failure of parts they have installed, if the parts are not new and warranted by the manufacturer. You can see their point here: there is no way to determine the serviceable life span of a used auto part. But second and more to the point, the mechanic makes a major part of his income by charging you a large markup on the new part, a markup that is not possible if he sold you used or rebuilt parts.

If you do your own car repairs, however, don't overlook the wreckage yard as a source of car parts at a savings. I have bought everything from used engines to third members (otherwise known as the differential, or "rear end"). Hubcaps, used tires (be careful here, because of the safety factor associated with tires, i.e., traction and stopping or braking power), alternators, radiators, batteries, and a host of other parts can be purchased from the salvage/wreckage yards, at considerable savings.

Many purveyors of used car parts will offer some sort of modified warranty, usually offering to replace a part if it fails within some reasonable period of time. Long-established salvage usually have some sort of reputation for fair dealings, but the best procedure is to check with friends or fellow workers to find a dealer who deals honestly.

Auto parts stores also offer recycled products in the form of rebuilt parts. Auto engines and transmissions can be purchased as rebuilts, or you can have your own "drive train" parts rebuilt if they are only worn but not damaged. Other parts, especially ignition parts such as alternators and generators, are perfectly serviceable when rebuilt, because "rebuilding" usually consists of replacing a few key components plus cleaning and testing.

For recycled auto parts, check in the Yellow Pages, under the heading "Auto Parts & Supplies."

CHECKLIST
CARS

❑ Read and heed your car's owner's manual. Do preventive maintenance steps at recommended intervals to get all the service your car can deliver.

❑ Keep tires properly inflated and balanced for better mileage, less wear.

❑ Have front end alignment checked when you buy a new car. Alignment often is badly adjusted at the factory. Have alignment checked if you hit a curb or pothole, or if front tires begin to wear unevenly.

❑ Keep the car exterior clean and polished. This will preserve the finish, prevent body rust damage, and reduce wind drag on the car.

❑ To avoid glass replacement, have chips in windshields repaired by Novus or a similar repair service. Neglected chips can become irreparable cracks, with glass replacement the only remaining option.

❑ Keep your car's engine tuned for better mileage and less air pollution.

❑ Use the lowest octane gas you can, as long as your engine does not "ping." It takes more petroleum to make a gallon of premium gas than to make regular or unleaded gas, and premium gas does not increase your car's gas mileage.

❑ To extend the life of your car, change the major fluids as recommended in your owner's manual. Failure to flush and replace old antifreeze can damage your car's cooling system; dirty oil can damage the engine; and automatic transmission fluid should be changed, along with the filter, per the manufacturer's recommendations.

❑ If you live in a climate where winter roads are salted, wash your car once a week. Salt is highly corrosive and will attack the underside of your car's body. Be particularly careful to clean the slush and road salt that clings in the car fenders and causes rust problems.

❑ Buy high-mileage tires and heavy-duty batteries to reduce the disposal problems these components generate.

❑ Avoid using additives such as mileage enhancers, stop-leak chemicals, or other fluids that claim to improve your car's life or performance. Premium oil and gas require no chemical additives.

8
Reducing Home Maintenance

For many years, as a contractor and later as a home writer, I have preached the gospel of quality and low maintenance. While we as individuals cannot do much about controlling the primary cost of housing, we can indeed do much to control the cost of living in that housing, i.e., repairs and maintenance. By making judicious buying decisions, we can install in our homes those products that last longest and require the least repair or maintenance.

CHOOSING MATERIALS

When I started in the building business, asphalt roof shingles lasted about fifteen years, maximum. With improved technology, the warranties were extended to twenty years, then to thirty years. Fiberglass mats, ceramic granules, and other improvements permitted us to double the life of the shingle. By using these top-grade shingles, we will be exposed to the replacement cost every thirty years, and only half as many shingles are generated into the annual waste stream, simply because the shingle lasts twice as long.

Keep in mind that the cost of using quality materials is only the cost differential between the good/better shingles themselves; the labor rate is constant. That is, it takes as much time to install cheap shingles, siding, or windows as it does to install premium grades that will last longer and per-

form better. The same is true of paint, carpet, wall covering, cabinets, plumbing fixtures, and lighting. Quality does not cost, it pays; and if one is concerned about the environment the payment is twofold. It is simple arithmetic that a product that lasts twice as long generates only half as much waste.

Windows today are designed with double pane, low-E glass for better energy conservation, plus vinyl or aluminum exterior cladding that helps the window resist rot and warping while reducing or eliminating painting and other such maintenance chores. If you're planning to build or remodel, buy the best windows you can find, for less maintenance and lower energy bills.

Low maintenance siding choices are also available. Masonry finishes such as stucco, brick, and stone don't require painting, and other maintenance is minimal. Stucco, for example, should not be painted, but may need periodic recoating with cement-based stucco products (this is known as redashing). Stone and brick may require repointing (repairing the mortar joints between stone or bricks) but will require no further attention, save for an occasional power washing.

Other siding choices for low maintenance are aluminum or steel and vinyl sidings. These can be applied directly over old siding, and will not need painting for twenty years or longer. When aluminum siding does need repainting, for example, the paint coating will usually last longer, because properly applied paint will last longer on the metal surface than on wood. Check with your paint dealer: most quality latex paints are recommended for recoating aluminum or steel siding. Aluminum or vinyl covering can also protect the overhang or soffit areas of your house, and can cover porch ceilings and fascia or roof trim boards. These areas, highly vulnerable to paint peeling and decay, benefit from these more permanent finishes.

Vinyl or aluminum shutters will look better longer, be less subject to paint peeling and warping, and are usually inexpensive to buy. Steel or fiberglass insulated doors conserve energy, resist warping and cracking, and can be as attractive as wood doors.

INSIDE THE HOME

Inside the house, buy appliances for their durability. Check manufacturers' warranties, or check with a testing agency such as *Consumer Reports* for frequency of repair. With appliance service calls becoming increasingly expensive, it is prudent to pay for quality up front. One high service bill can wipe out any "savings" you might have gained through lower purchasing price. This approach in business is called "life cycle costing," meaning that the *real* cost of an item is a combination of purchasing price, operating costs, and repair costs over the lifetime of the item. The message can be seen in the old Maytag appliance commercials that show their repairman as the "loneliest guy in town."

Save the owner's operating manual on all new appliances. Note whether the appliance is lifetime-lubricated, or whether it needs periodic lubrication. Keep all appliances clean, and keep the cabinets waxed. A coat of automotive paste wax will protect the finish on appliances such as clothes washers and dryers, and help prevent rust. Don't overlook the cabinet on your furnace and hot wa-

ter heater: appliances that are located in the basement are especially subject to rust.

One of the most important and oft-overlooked chores is periodic replacement of the furnace filter. On a forced-air furnace, the filter should be replaced monthly during the heating season. If the furnace also combines central air, replace the filter each month during summer cooling. The filter not only keeps the blower and furnace clean, it also keeps the air ducts dirt-free. An astronomical amount of money is spent on cleaning and redecorating, just to clean interiors that have been soiled by household dirt blown through the heating/air conditioning system. Change the filter to keep interior air clean, and you'll spend far less time cleaning and far less money for cleaning products that add to the waste stream.

Most of the dirt and grit that damages the home and its carpet and floor coverings enters the house on the shoes of family members or guests. Keep large, commercial-type mats at all entry doors, and ask people to wipe their feet before entering. Even better, place a rack full of house slippers at entry points, and ask entrants to remove street shoes before entering the house.

Use a powerful vacuum cleaner to vacuum room rugs and carpets. Sand and grit that is tracked onto carpets will sink to the backing and cut carpet fibers. Use an electric broom to clean vinyl, tile, or wood floors before grit can scratch and mar the finish.

When shopping for floor covering, choose no-wax vinyl floor covering. Choose premium carpets with superior stain resistance and construction, such as Armstrong World Industries, Inc.'s Stainmaster® Carpet. For prefinished hardwood flooring, Bruce offers floor finishes of polyurethane that resist abrasion and need no waxing.

Ceramic tile can last forever, if it is properly installed and periodically maintained. The chief offense with ceramic tile is failure to grout the cracks. If water is permitted to penetrate behind the tile, the tile will eventually fail, and you'll have a whole dumpster full of expensive bathroom to add to the waste stream. Wipe tile, tub, and shower down with your bath towel when you've finished bathing, and the tile and fixtures will last longer and require fewer cleaning products to keep them sparkling.

Quality cabinets, durable wood paneling, and hardwood moldings and trim all should last the life of the house if they are not abused. If you have an older house with darkened stain, don't assume you have to paint it. First, check to see if you can clean the grime off the dark wood and reveal a fine varnish finish underneath. Wipe the woodwork with a clean cloth soaked in odorless mineral spirits to remove old wax and dirt buildup.

Modern wall coverings can also last a lifetime. Choose vinyls that can be cleaned and that will not absorb dirt or grease. Interior latex paints are inexpensive, easy to apply, and contribute little to pollution. Some latex paints contain mercury (more often used in exterior paints, as a mildewcide), but paint companies are starting to note on labels whether their paints contain mercury, so be selective.

REMODELING

In addition to buying quality building materials and appliances, you can also affect the waste flow by considering the effect of remodeling projects. If possible, leave old materials in place, and cover over them, rather than removing them for disposal. For example, if you decide to finish off attic space, the present ceiling insulation will not contribute to energy savings, because it will now be between two heated spaces. (Insulation only saves energy when it is positioned between conditioned space and exterior temperatures: insulation between a cold garage and the exterior adds little value, because insulation is a barrier to heat flow,

and there is no heat to conserve in an unheated garage.) You must place new insulation between the newly finished attic space and the roof. Regardless, you should leave the old insulation in place. It will serve a minor role as soundproofing, and it is messy to remove it and dispose of it.

The same advice is true of old plaster. Have a pro check the walls and ceilings to see if they are still sound and capable of being repaired. The criteria here is that the plaster is still tightly adhered to the lath backer, and is not hanging loose and unsupported. If the plaster is still stuck tight to the lath it can be repaired and patched, thus keeping it in service. If the plaster is loose from the lath on a ceiling, you may be able to nail furring strips over the old plaster, then screw wallboard to the furring strips. For walls that are badly damaged, consider placing wallboard over the old plaster, giving the wall a new surface or "skin." Use 3/8-inch thick wallboard to resurface over old plaster. This may require the expertise of a professional contractor, because adding to the thickness of the walls means removing the trim, installing spacers on the window and door frames, then replacing the trim molding. Only as a last resort should you remove the old plaster, because the tons of plaster and lath will cause a mess, be expensive to remove, and will add to the trash that clogs landfills.

Experts from the U.S. Environmental Protection Agency (EPA) advise that asbestos is best simply left alone. This is true because the dangerous factor with asbestos is the airborne particles. If asbestos is solid, not crumbling, leave it alone rather than remove it. The removal may create more problems than it solves.

The same is true for old siding, with qualifications. Siding replacement time is an excellent time to upgrade sidewall insulation. You can choose to leave the siding in place and apply foam board insulation over the old siding, then apply the new siding over the foam insulation board. Or you can remove the old siding and discard it. This step lets you open up the wall cavities and place insulation in them. This approach is much more effective than trying to "blow" or "pump" new insulation into the space with the siding intact, for the obvious reason that you can see how completely the insulation is filling the cavities, and avoid any misses or gaps. You can then apply foam board as an insulating sheathing over the walls, then install the new siding. The drawback to this approach is the labor to remove the old siding and the job of disposing of it. The same is true of window replacement: writers like me often urge you to replace the old windows for energy efficiency but fail to point out one little problem: many landfills will not accept old windows because of the glass problem. Be sure you have a disposal area that will accept the old windows before you replace them.

Roof shingles are another headache. You can leave one layer of asphalt shingles in place and add another layer atop the first. But your local codes will require that you remove the shingles, both layers, down to bare roof sheathing, when that second layer is ready for replacement. Here again, two layers of old shingles will fill a dumpster, so thirty-year shingles can make life much easier.

Additions to the house and backyard projects such as decks will also benefit from good planning, to avoid waste and disposal problems. For example, I added a ground level addition to my deck. The project was featured in *Workbench Magazine*. The thrust of the story was that I used all pressure-treated lumber, all in 12-foot lengths. With advance planning I made exactly two saw cuts (to make steps from the new deck level up to the old deck) and generated no waste or cutoff lumber. By handpicking the deck boards to avoid split lumber and pieces with loose knots, I was able to do the project with absolutely no waste. Try to plan your project for maximum energy conservation, with as little future maintenance as possible, to avoid adding to the pollution and waste disposal problems.

RECYCLING APPLIANCES

If bans on dumping certain items have not yet appeared in your area, they soon will be. Bans on dumping appliances are already on the way, for those who are not already so restricted. My home state of Minnesota has already passed such a ban. We can no longer include appliances in our regular trash pickups, or haul appliances to landfills or to any other solid waste processing facility.

In place of dumping appliances we must now ship them to licensed appliance recyclers. In most cases, the dealer who sells you a new, replacement appliance will arrange for pickup and disposal of the old appliance.

The ban covers new major appliances such as washers, dryers, freezers and refrigerators, air conditioners, ranges and conventional ovens, dishwashers, water heaters, and garbage disposals. Appliances cannot be easily crushed for burial, will not burn if mixed into trash at a waste/energy incinerator, but do contain metals and plastics that can be recycled. The appliance recycler will usually attempt to repair appliances for reuse, the ultimate recycling.

If the appliance cannot be repaired, the recycler must try to recover any harmful chemicals. Some switches may contain mercury; capacitors on older appliance motors can contain PCBs, a hazardous material; the Freon® in cooling appliances is a suspected hazard to the ozone layer.

CHECKLIST

REDUCING HOME MAINTENANCE

❏ Choose building and remodeling products with an eye to future maintenance costs. Select prefinished siding (aluminum, vinyl); look for thirty-year warranties on roofing; buy house paint with a fifteen-year warranty to reduce work, cost, and hazards to the environment.

❏ Read consumer surveys and testing reports and use them as a guide for buying appliances. Watch the "frequency of repair" rating to avoid frequent repair bills.

❏ Trim back trees and shrubs that shade siding or roofing. Materials do not dry out after a rain if they are in shade, and rot and mildew can result.

❏ Buy a hole punch and a two-ring binder notebook. When you buy an appliance, punch holes in the warranty and owner's manual and place them in the notebook for quick reference.

❏ Save, read, and heed owner's maintenance and repair manuals on appliances and cars to get the most for your dollars.

❏ Check whether your furnace blower motor and the compressor on your air conditioner need oiling. If they do, buy an engineer's oiler with a flexible spout and oil motors as directed in owner's manuals.

❏ Keep ceramic tile grouted and the tub/tile joint caulked to prevent tile failure and expensive water damage to the wall.

❏ Keep a remodeling/maintenance diary on your home, so you can have the information (how old is the furnace, when did we re-roof?) handy. The diary can be presented to new owners when you sell your home.

❏ Patch holes and cracks in blacktop (asphalt) or concrete drives and walks to prevent buckling and major cracking.

❏ Seal concrete and asphalt drives or slabs. Sealed surfaces prevent water entry; prevent dusting on concrete floors, garage floors, and patios; and make an easy task of wiping up oil or other spills before they can penetrate and stain the slab.

❏ Keep furnace filters clean. Place oversized mats at entry doors so people don't track in dirt. Don't smoke inside. Your cleaning, decorating, and dry cleaning bills will plummet.

❏ Put various screwdrivers and a penetrating/lubricating product such as WD-40® in a basket. Mark a Saturday morning, once a year, on your maintenance calendar. Remove, clean, and lubricate all hinges and locks in your house to keep them operating smoothly.

❏ Buy washable paint and wall covering. Buy no-wax vinyl flooring and carpeting with a stain guard. Have all your upholstered furniture treated with Scotchgard®, and it will resist staining and be easy to clean.

9
Hazardous Waste

When we think of conservation and recycling, we may think of overflowing landfills, or the need to return aluminum cans to waste recyclers. We think of hazardous wastes as being those that are generated by businesses or industries such as nuclear power stations. But the increase in home use of dangerous chemicals has accelerated since the end of World War II, and household disposal problems now include how to dispose of waste products that are dangerous to humans, pets, or the environment. This chapter deals with how to avoid buying and using hazardous chemicals and other products, and how to dispose of products that today may seem necessary or their use unavoidable.

CHARACTERISTICS OF HAZARDOUS PRODUCTS

Briefly, materials are deemed to be hazardous if they present some level of danger to our health or environment. The danger can arise when such materials or products are improperly used, stored, or disposed of. Materials that should be labeled as hazardous include:

- Materials that are flammable or explosive (gasoline, paint solvents, paint strippers)

- Acidic or caustic materials (muriatic acid for cleaning concrete and masonry, oven cleaners, paint strippers)

- Those items with a high degree of toxicity to humans or pets (pesticides, prescription drugs, auto antifreeze)

- Products that can react with water (acids) or explode from exposure to heat or pressure (aerosol containers)

- Materials that contribute oxygen or other flammable/explosive gases to a fire (hydrogen peroxide, adhesives)

Possible dangers from these hazardous wastes can arise from improper use, storage, or disposal. Some chemicals can cause an explosion when mixed together; ignoring label directions can lead to overuse or poisoning of the user (from failure to wear appropriate masks, eating or smoking without washing hands, or inhaling fumes from various products such as solvents). Remember, the fumes from toxic chemicals are toxic as well.

Storage of hazardous products is an uncertain proposition. Storage containers such as paper or kraft bags or metal cans may deteriorate in time and spill the hazardous materials. Spilled chemicals may be ingested by children or pets or may create a fire hazard.

Disposal likewise can create problems. Containers can deteriorate in landfills, releasing noxious materials into soil or ground water. In my state of Minnesota, the Pollution Control Agency estimates

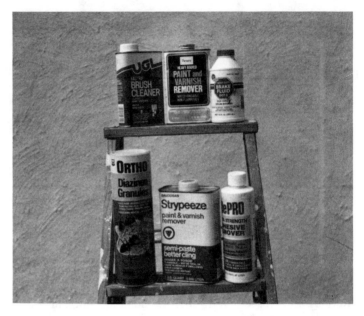

Common household chemicals such as insecticides, car brake fluid, paint remover, and solvents should be used only according to label directions, and the containers disposed of safely.

that as many as one-third of the state's landfills *are known* to be leaking and contaminating ground water. Solvents, oils, and auto wastes can leach into ground water or well water used for drinking. A high percentage of wells in Minnesota are contaminated by agricultural chemicals such as fertilizers, pesticides, and herbicides.

If you live in an area that has sanitary sewers, be aware that some chemicals may pass through the treatment and into the ocean or a river. Chemicals that are flushed into septic systems may leach into wells or underground aquifers, or may kill bacteria that are necessary to break down sewage wastes.

Storm sewers pick up runoff water from rain or melting snow and dump it untreated directly into a nearby lake, river, or ocean. This direct dumping of water that should be relatively clean saves the cost of treatment that must be done to the contents of the sanitary sewer. But it is necessary for us to understand that only rain or snow melt should go into these untreated systems. As pointed out in Chapter 7, oil and transmission leaks are washed from streets and highways directly into rivers and lakes. Herbicides and pesticides from lawns also wash into storm sewers or any water standing nearby.

The best way to reduce the problem of hazardous wastes is to practice source reduction or "precycling." When facing a particular problem, try to take the least polluting route to solving the problem. This may mean buying rechargeable batteries rather than buying the disposable, throwaway batteries, or caulking cracks to keep bugs out of the house instead of using an aerosol spray pesticide product to kill insects after they enter.

- Look for non-polluting alternatives when you buy.

- Buy only enough to do the job.

- Apply the product at its intended level as indicated on the label.

- Use the product up or give it to someone who will use it.

- Dispose of the empty container in a safe manner.

Remember, the best way to solve the problem of

hazardous waste is not to buy hazardous products. When you cannot avoid using hazardous products, follow label directions carefully, to avoid danger to your family and pollution to the environment. Do not mix hazardous chemicals together for disposal because you might get a volatile or dangerous chemical reaction. Finally, leave the material in the container in which it was purchased and leave the label intact. This way, you or disposal experts can easily identify the product and dispose of it properly.

In other chapters, we have talked about disposal methods for various materials, from paint to auto fluids. Because we believe that this advice bears repeating, and to advise how to dispose of other household chemicals not yet dealt with, we will summarize the instructions on how to dispose of hazardous wastes that are commonly used in the home.

PAINTS

Paints are usually divided into two types: water-base (latex) paints and oil-base paints, which is a catch-all category for virtually any paint product that is not latex: enamels, alkyds, varnishes, shellacs, stains, and sealers are all included in this category.

The test of whether a paint product is latex is whether it can be thinned or cleaned up with water only. If water is the only solvent needed, then the product is latex. If alcohol (shellac), lacquer thinner (lacquers), or mineral spirits (alkyds and enamels) must be used for thinning or for cleaning tools, the product is not latex-based. Whenever a latex-based product is available for the job at hand, choose latexes over oil paints as being generally less hazardous to your family and to the environment. Some exterior latex paints contain mercury, which is used as a mildewcide. Check paint labels to be sure your paint choice does not contain mercury.

The greatest danger from paint disposal may be disposing of paint in its liquid form. The liquid paint chemicals may mix with water or other chemicals and be carried down to underground aquifers to pollute ground water. This is the reason that most landfills bar dumping of any liquids, from paints to waste oil. Many trash haulers will not pick up leftover paint in liquid form. When paint cans are compacted or flattened in the dump or landfill, the lids can pop off, releasing the liquid paint to flow where it will.

Try to buy paint in limited quantities, only enough to do the job at hand. If some paint is left over, give one wall an extra coat to rid yourself of the paint, or use it to paint a closet. You can mix leftover portions of paint, assuming the leftovers are all compatible; i.e., latex or water base, or those that can be thinned with the same solvent, such as mineral spirits. Avoid using paint colors that are hard to dispose of. Mixing most colors together will eventually yield a color that is known in the construction industry as "builders' beige," a color that is not unattractive when used in closets or storage areas, finished garages, workshops, and the like.

If you cannot use up leftover paint, offer to give it to anyone who can use it. Relatives, neighbors, churches, community centers, and theater departments of schools can all use odd paint lots. Many charitable organizations will accept leftover paint, but in most cases will accept no less than one-half gallon lots.

If paint has been stored for months or years, check to see if it is still usable before trying to give it away. In old paint, pigment settles to the bottom of the can. If you can stir the pigment back into the paint, it is probably still usable. Never use old paint that contains lead.

The last resort is to discard the paint. The trick here is to let the paint dry out so it is no longer liquid. Remove the lid from the paint can and let the liquid portion evaporate. Do this only in a

Check local guidelines for disposal of liquid hazardous wastes. If there is no waste disposal facility near you, place a plastic bag inside a cardboard box, fill the bag with kitty litter, and pour small amounts of the product into the absorbent material. Do this in an open area. Let the waste dry or evaporate, then seal the plastic bag, close the box, and dispose of the package with the trash.

well-ventilated area, preferably in a locked porch or a garden shed with good ventilation. Note that the fumes of toxic materials are toxic, so it is very important to have plenty of ventilation and keep the materials away from people and pets.

If there is only a small amount of paint in a gallon can, leaving the lid off will probably be enough to let the liquid evaporate and the paint harden.

Both oil and latex paints will first "skim over," or form a solid film on top of the liquid paint. Use a paint stirring stick to cut through the solid film and let air reach the paint to ensure that all liquids evaporate before you discard the paint can.

Always check with local authorities for instructions on discarding hazardous materials. In most areas you can roll leftover paint onto cardboard or newspapers to get rid of it. You can also place a plastic garbage or yard bag in a cardboard box, pour a layer of paint onto the plastic, and let the paint setup. Then pour another thin layer of paint on top of the first layer, let it dry, then keep adding layers of paint until you have spread and dried all the paint. Be sure all paint is dried and hardened before discarding.

Stains, which are often made of little pigment or solids, with most of the volume being solvent, are difficult to dry up. Evaporating a material that is chiefly solvent may take too long. For these materials, consider placing a layer of absorbent material, such as kitty litter or the oil absorbent sold in auto parts stores, in a cardboard box lined with a plastic trash bag. Then pour the leftover stain into the kitty litter, mixing the liquid in slowly to be sure it is all absorbed. When the stain is fully absorbed by the kitty litter and the smell has diminished (meaning that the solvent has evaporated), place the absorbent and stain in a plastic bag and seal the bag before discarding it in the trash.

CAUTIONS: Be sure all solvent has evaporated; the solvent may cause a fire by spontaneous combustion. Be sure to handle and dry all solvent in open air to minimize danger of fire or from inhalation of the fumes.

SOLVENTS

A dictionary definition of the word solvent includes its ability to dissolve another material. Solvents may be liquid or aerosol products used to dissolve grease or oil when cleaning auto parts, for example. Solvents can also be used for cleaning grease from clothes or hands, for thinning paint or cleaning paint tools, or for stripping paints.

The best way to deal with solvents is to avoid the need to use them. Buying latex paint products will eliminate the need to buy paint thinners or mineral spirits, which would be needed to thin or clean up oil-base paints.

If you must use a product that requires a solvent, try reusing the solvent as much as possible. For example, degreasing solvents can be poured into a container, and auto parts or other objects can be cleaned in the solvent.

After cleaning or degreasing the parts, remove them and let the solvent sit in the container until the grease and dirt have settled to the bottom of the container. Then carefully pour off the clean solvent into another container for reuse. Place the sediment container in the open air where the solvent can evaporate, then dispose of the sediment in your trash.

The same advice can be used for dealing with oil-base paint solvents. Clean the brushes or rollers in the solvent, then let the container sit undisturbed so the paint residue will settle to the bottom of the container. Carefully, so as not to disturb the paint residue, pour off the clear solvent into another container, and put a lid on the container so the solvent will not evaporate. Leave the residue in the container and set the container in the open air, where the solvent remaining can evaporate. Then remove the dried sludge from the container and dispose of it with your other trash.

When handling solvents, keep in mind that they can be hazardous to eyes, skin, and lungs. Wear long-sleeved shirts to cover your arms, rubber gloves for your hands, and goggles to protect your eyes. Handle solvents only in open air or wear an approved mask. Wash your hands thoroughly be-fore eating, drinking, or smoking to avoid ingesting the solvents. Remember: The fumes from toxic materials are toxic.

There are two types of solvents, and disposal methods vary between the types. The product label will tell you what kind you have.

Chlorinated Solvents

The first type of solvent is chlorinated solvent, or one that contains chlorine. Check the label ingredient list for any mention of "chloro," "chlor," or "chloride." Examples might be "methylene chloride," "carbon tetrachloride," or "trichloroethylene." Chlorinated solvents may include dry cleaning products such as perchloroethylene, paint strippers, or degreasing products such as trichloroethylene.

To dispose of chlorinated solvents, first try to use them up or give them to someone who can use them. An example might be to give leftover paint stripper to a friend whose hobby is refinishing furniture, or even a shop where furniture is stripped or rebuilt.

If you cannot find any alternative, line a cardboard box with plastic and fill the box with kitty litter or driveway oil absorbent material. Carefully — avoid breathing the fumes — pour *up to one quart* of the solvent into the absorbent. Leave the box open, outdoors, so the solvent can evaporate, then discard the box and its contents with your other trash.

To dispose of solvents in aerosol containers, place an empty cardboard box outdoors, in the open air. Shake the aerosol container well and completely empty the solvent from the aerosol can, spraying the contents into the cardboard box. Let the solvent evaporate, then discard the box and the aerosol container with your other trash.

Note that the instructions here are for disposing of small amounts of chlorinated solvents. For larger amounts of solvent, contact local authorities or your Environmental Protection Agency office for instructions on disposal.

Be aware also that chlorinated products such as paint strippers can damage your forced-air furnace equipment. The note to "use with adequate ventilation" in fact means to use them *only* where ventilation is equal to being outdoors. If fumes containing chlorine are drawn into the combustion chamber of a forced-air furnace, the chlorine can combine with hydrogen to form hydrochloric acid (HCL), which can quickly destroy the heat exchanger of the furnace.

Non-Chlorinated Solvents

The second type of solvent is the non-chlorinated solvent. These solvents usually have a petroleum or alcohol base and are often labeled "combustible" or "flammable." Non-chlorinated solvents include mineral spirits and paint thinners, toluene, acetone, methanol (wood alcohol), and lacquer thinner. Again, observe safety precautions when handling any solvents.

Many non-chlorinated solvents can be poured into the sanitary sewer (not into septic systems, however). Alcohol solvents such as methanol (wood alcohol), isopropanol (common rubbing alcohol), and ethanol (grain alcohol) can be flushed down sewer drains, along with acetone (nail polish remover, also used as a solvent for "crazy glues") and methyl ethyl ketone (MEK). Remember that these products may be flammable and their fumes may be toxic. Handle them with care and flush away with plenty of water.

Non-chlorinated solvents such as mineral spirits, paint thinners, and lacquer thinners cannot be poured into sewers. Instead, pour the solvents into a box lined with plastic and filled with kitty litter. Let the fumes evaporate, then discard the box in the trash. The homeowner should not, if he or she is a careful shopper, accumulate large amounts of these solvents. If you do have more than one gal-

lon of non-chlorinated solvent to dispose of, contact your local experts such as the Pollution Control Agency or Environmental Protection Agency for disposal instructions.

PESTICIDES

In Chapter 3, "Lawn and Garden," we discussed ways of avoiding chemical pesticides. Good gardening practices, combined with the development of non-toxic pesticides, should virtually eliminate toxic pesticides from lawn and garden use. To be sure you need a pesticide, you can contact the local agricultural extension service of the Department of Agriculture or your local hardware store.

Exploring Alternatives to Pesticides

Many types of pesticides are available for dealing with household pests. Roach and ant aerosol sprays, poison products for mice, and various other fly and bug killers abound. What alternatives can we use for interior pesticides? First of all, insects and others pests need an entry point to get into the house. Do a really careful check of your home's exterior and caulk or weatherstrip every crack you can find. Watch the house exterior: you will often see a parade of ants or other insects marching toward an open hole or crack in the house's exterior. Seal these entry points and check them every spring to be sure the caulk has not cracked or washed away.

Next, keep door and window screens in good repair. Replace damaged screens to prevent insects and other pests from entering.

Inside the house, caulk all cracks and crevices where insects might enter or hide. Cockroaches, for example, like tight quarters and live in tiny cracks where they actually feel pressure, according to tests done at Johnson Wax laboratories. Fill all such cracks to discourage pests and eliminate their hideouts.

Another pest requirement is water. Fix any leaking or dripping pipes, especially those under sinks in cabinets, where the insects can find water, food, and shelter. If you make an uncomfortable environment for pests they will seek other quarters. Remove stacks of newspapers, old magazines, and other refuse that provides shelter to pests.

Don't overlook the food requirements of pests. Clean up any food spills immediately, reseal opened boxes, and place food in pest-proof containers such as Tupperware®. Again, pests won't linger where there is no food. Don't leave pet food in the bowl after feeding, where it will attract flies and other insects.

When There is No Alternative . . .

If you cannot avoid using pesticides, buy small quantities, follow label application directions, and store leftover product safely until it can be used up. When you have used all the product, rinse the container thoroughly, and use the pesticide/rinse water to avoid dumping the water into drains.

If you are moving or cannot use up all the pesticide, offer to donate it to a garden club, church, or greenhouse, and use the disposal only as a last resort. Pesticides in powder form can be left in their containers, wrapped in several layers of newspaper, then placed inside a double plastic bag for disposal in the trash.

Don't discard liquid pesticides (or any liquid product) in the trash, where it may end up in a landfill and has the potential to reach ground water. Instead, pour liquid pesticide over kitty litter (in a cardboard box double-lined with plastic) so it is absorbed; then seal the bag before disposing of it.

AEROSOLS

Aerosol products have often been the target of criticism, sometimes undeserved. Aerosol products can offer spill-proof packaging and precise application, so they actually can reduce the amount of product used. For example, the spray wand that can be attached to the nozzle of the aerosol can will provide pinpoint accuracy in delivering a solvent or lubricant precisely where it is need, with no waste. Aerosol paint products provide the consumer with a delivery system (spraying) that could otherwise be done only with expensive air compressors. Auto touchup paint, for example, could, in the long run, reduce environmental damage (from damaged and discarded cars) by protecting auto bodies from rust.

The arguments against using aerosols arise from the potential damage that allegedly comes from aerosol propellants. For this reason the aerosol industry quit using fluorocarbons as a propellant, except in rare instances such as inhalant products for asthmatics. The other objection to aerosol products is their potential explosive hazard if they are used, stored, or discarded improperly. The consumer can alleviate most problems by using aerosol products properly and disposing of the containers in an approved fashion.

First of all, consider options to using aerosol products. Many common cosmetic products, such as deodorants, are available in other forms such as roll-on tubes. On the other hand, such common products as aerosol paints cannot be applied in other ways, so elimination of all aerosol products is probably not possible or even desirable.

As with most products, however, there are proper ways of using, storing, and disposing of aerosol products. The first rule is always to read and observe any label instructions.

Some aerosol products can be dangerous if used near fire or flames: paint, solvents, and lubricants may be included on this list. Never use aerosol products near heat or flames or while smoking. Always use aerosol maintenance products with adequate ventilation; i.e., outdoors or in a ventilated area such as an enclosed porch.

Spray aerosol products such as paints or solvents into a cardboard box. Let dry. Be sure to discharge the entire contents of the aerosol can, including the propellant. When the fluid contents have dried, place the box in the trash.

Next, observe storage precautions for aerosol products. Remember that the products are under pressure, so avoid storing auto products in the trunk during hot weather, when the heat buildup could cause them to rupture or to explode with force. The same is true for shop storage: keep aerosol cans in a place where room temperatures are normal.

Use up all the aerosol product before you discard the container, but go even further. Shake the can well and void all the propellant before discarding the can. It is the propellant remaining in the can that makes the explosion hazard, and all or most products caution the user to deplete the propellant before discarding the can.

A common complaint of consumers is that the nozzle on the aerosol can become clogged, so all the contents cannot be voided. This is especially true of spray paint cans, because paint dries quickly and clogs the nozzle. Observe the recommendation on the aerosol can to turn the can upside down and spray a burst of propellant through the paint nozzle before putting the can away. The propellant will thus clear the nozzle of paint residue. If you have a nozzle that is already clogged, soak it in the appropriate solvent or brush cleaner to clear the nozzle. Also, nozzles from paint cans are often interchangeable, so if one is clogged you can remove it and use a like nozzle to empty the aerosol can. Use caution when working with aerosol spray products. Work in open air to avoid breathing the fumes, and wash hands and face before eating or smoking.

To dispose of aerosol containers, spray the product into a cardboard box and let any solvent evaporate. Again, be sure to keep spraying after the product is gone, to remove the propellant — and the pressure — from the container. This will eliminate the danger of an explosion that might injure a sanitation worker. When the aerosol can is empty, discard it in the trash. Remember, the best way to avoid pollution from hazardous materials is always to use the product up, for its intended purpose, before disposing of the container.

ANTIFREEZE

Several hazardous products are fluids used in your

car. Antifreeze is one such product, but if it is properly disposed of it need not be a problem. The chemicals in antifreeze can be neutralized in a sewage treatment plant, so it is safe to pour *small amounts* down the sewer drain. Note that we are talking about city sewer systems; antifreeze can damage or destroy the bacterial action needed in a septic system, so never pour antifreeze into a septic system. Pour used antifreeze slowly into a sink, drain, or toilet, and use plenty of water to flush and dilute the antifreeze.

Remember, too, that you should not drain antifreeze directly onto the ground or drive, where it can be washed into storm sewers. Water picked up by storm sewers is untreated, so you are dumping raw antifreeze directly into the lake or river. Nor should you allow drained antifreeze to puddle. Antifreeze has a sweet taste that attracts pets, and cats and dogs are often poisoned by this product.

The good news as we write this is that new machines will clean the old antifreeze, add rustproofers and other chemicals that are depleted with age, then return the cleaned product to your radiator, thus reducing the impact of antifreeze on our environment.

OIL

Waste oil from cars, recreation equipment, and yard and garden tractors and tools can pollute water and soil if improperly disposed of. There is also some evidence that motor oil that comes in contact with bare skin may cause skin cancer if not promptly cleaned off. If you do your own car maintenance, keep your skin covered, clean up any oil spills promptly, and catch the oil in a container so that it can be recycled.

Waste oil can be recycled for use as an industrial fuel or it can be re-refined and used again as a lubricant. Until the 1960s service stations often offered a choice between their own brand of new oil and glass bottles of re-refined oils for about half the price of new oil. Many people who owned older "oil-burner" cars would buy the cheaper oil, because they had to add a quart every few hundred miles. However, a neighbor of mine in those years owned and operated a business that collected and re-refined oil, and he used his own re-refined oil in all his cars and fleet of trucks. This neighbor often boasted that his re-refined oil was actually better in a car engine than new oil, because the first customer had removed harmful varnish material from the oil with its first use. Whether this claim had any scientific basis I cannot prove. I do know the neighbor had a fleet of business vehicles that appeared to thrive on the used oil, with no apparent engine problems from using re-refined oil.

It is a fact that oil does not "wear out"; it must be changed because it picks up dirt and contaminants while being pumped through the car engine.

Waste oil is a valuable and reusable resource. In many communities, businesses that sell motor oil must accept the used oil for recycling or direct customers — via posted directions — to a business that will accept used oil for recycling. Many service stations sell their used oil to recyclers who pick the oil up on a periodic basis. These stations often let you leave your waste oil for recycling.

Change your motor oil only when it is dirty or at the intervals recommended by the manufacturer. Use quality oil filters on your cars or trucks to keep oil clean and extend its life. When you must change oil, pour the used oil into plastic gallon jugs (milk jugs, antifreeze jugs, or bleach jugs — any container with a good, tight-fitting cap) and seal the jug with the cap. Deposit the used oil at the nearest service station or oil recycling center. And check the underside of your car frequently, to be sure the car is not leaking oil. Oil that drips onto the roadway is washed by rain into storm sewers, and the storm sewers dump the raw oil directly into lakes and rivers.

WOOD PRESERVATIVES

Wood preservatives work in one of two ways. Some preservatives contain chemicals that are toxic to organisms that attack wood and cause decay. Some preservatives may simply contain chemicals that block water entry with its attendant wood rot, splitting, and decay.

The best way to avoid pollution from wood preservatives is to use them up on outdoor projects such as fences, decks, and mailbox posts.

If you have any wood preservative on hand, check the label for ingredients. Look for any mention of creosote or pentachlorophenol. The Environmental Protection Agency has declared that any preservative containing either of those chemicals should not be handled by any person(s) who have not had special training in proper handling. If you have any preservative that contains either of these chemicals, try to dispose of them by offering them to landscaping or nursery firms.

If you have no more than one quart of preservative which contains creosote, fill a plastic yard bag with kitty litter, and pour the preservative onto the litter. Wear gloves and cover your arms when handling creosote because it can burn the skin. Be sure you have enough kitty litter to completely absorb all the liquid, then seal the bag and dispose of it in your trash.

There is no accepted method for disposing of preservatives that contain pentachlorophenol. If you cannot give it to professional handlers, store it in a safe area until you can find an acceptable disposal method recommended by your local government.

Pressure-treated Lumber

About ten years ago pressure-treated lumber came on the consumer scene. Because lesser species of lumber could be utilized when pressure treated, the product reduced the need for cutting more desirable species of trees, such as red cedar and redwood. Using pressure-treated lumber allowed us to use our timber resources more fully, and because the lumber was somewhat less expensive than either redwood or cedar, its popularity grew quickly.

Most pressure-treated lumber has been treated with an EPA-registered pesticide to protect the lumber from decay and insect attack. The common chemical used is inorganic arsenic, which may present hazards for homeowners who come into contact with it if it is not properly handled. You should follow and observe certain precautions when handling or disposing of treated wood.

Use pressure-treated lumber only where such protection is necessary, for exterior projects and for any wood that will be in contact with the ground. You may use pressure-treated wood indoors provided you carefully clean up and dispose of all sawdust and scrap lumber after your project is finished. Pressure-treated wood is commonly used for all-weather wood foundations, for example.

Before using pressure-treated wood for patios, sidewalks, or decks, be sure it is clean and free of any treatment residue. Do not use treated lumber where it will have direct contact with drinking water. You can, of course, use pressure-treated lumber for docks or decks on waterways.

Do not use pressure-treated lumber for storing food for farm animals, such as in silos, nor for feed bunkers for cattle. Also, do not use pressure-treated lumber for any part of a beehive that might come in contact with honey.

When working with pressure-treated lumber, use normal precautions for personal sanitation. Wash hands thoroughly after handling the lumber and before eating, drinking, or smoking. Wear a dust mask when sawing lumber, and avoid breathing in sawdust from any wood. If treated wood feels wet to the touch, allow it to dry out before handling it. After working with pressure-treated wood, wash work clothes separately from family laundry.

Dispose of treated lumber scraps in the trash or bury them. Do not burn pressure-treated lumber in open fires, wood stoves, or fireplaces. The chemicals in the wood may prove toxic when released in smoke or ashes.

PRESCRIPTION DRUGS

Most outdated prescription or non-prescription drugs can be safely disposed of at home. You can safely flush most unused drugs down your sewer or septic system. Try to use up drugs as you buy them. Most prescriptions are written by the physician in the quantity intended for use. At your doctor's direction, use up all prescription medicines.

Most non-prescription drugs present no hazard to the environment and should be flushed down the toilet. One safety precaution for using drugs: never pick a dropped pill or capsule off the floor and swallow it. An old pharmacist stepped on dropped pills to crush them. His reason? You can't tell if the pill you pick up is the one you just dropped. There is the outside chance that the pill you see may be from someone else's prescription and may be hazardous to you.

One exception for dealing with disposal of drugs: you should not flush chemotherapy drugs down the toilet. Instead, ask your doctor, pharmacist, or local EPA office for advice on how to dispose of these powerful drugs.

COSMETICS

Most liquid cosmetics, such as colognes and perfumes, can be poured into the toilet or floor drain and flushed away. Solids such as face powders can be disposed of with regular trash. Disposing of nail polish remover, see the section on solvents.

HOUSEHOLD CLEANERS

As with most household products, the best way to deal with cleaners is to buy and use the products that are the least hazardous, use the products as directed on the label, and dispose of the product container as directed. If you are moving and do not want to move containers that have been opened, give the cleaners to a relative, neighbor, or church or other organization.

Most household cleaning products can be safely flushed down the toilet. Bleaches, window cleaners, ammonia products, and pine oil cleaners can be flushed down the toilet. Solid or paste products such as floor or car waxes and furniture polishes can be thrown away with regular household trash.

When cleaning or disposing of cleaning products, do not mix products that contain chlorine bleach with products containing ammonia. Bleach, toilet cleaners, and oven cleaners may give off toxic fumes if they are mixed with ammonia cleaners.

CHECKLIST
HAZARDOUS WASTE DISPOSAL

PRODUCT	HOW TO DISPOSE OF IT
Aerosols	Use up product or spray remainder into a cardboard box, spray out propellant, dispose of container and box in trash
Antifreeze	Sewer drain
Cleaning products, liquid	Bleaches, window cleaners, ammonia products, pine oil cleaners: flush down toilet
Cleaning products, solid	Waxes, polishes: place in trash
Cosmetics, liquid	Flush down toilet
Cosmetics, powder	Dispose in trash
Drugs, non-prescription	Flush down toilet
Drugs, prescription	Dispose of leftovers in sewer drain; do not flush chemotherapy drugs into drain — ask pharmacist for instructions
Engine oil	Recycle at service station
Paint, latex	Let dry out in can and throw away or spread on newspapers and throw away
Paint, oil-base	Give to church, charity, or theater or let dry up in can and throw away
Pesticides, liquid	Place absorbent material in double plastic trash bag, pour in liquid pesticide, seal bags and place in trash
Pesticides, powder	Wrap container(s) in newspapers, place inside plastic trash bag, seal, dispose of in trash
Pressure-treated lumber	Dispose of scraps in trash. Don't burn: may give off toxic ash
Solvents, chlorinated (check label for "chloro")	Pour into absorbent such as kitty litter, let evaporate, dispose of in trash
Solvents, non-chlorinated (not water-soluble)	Alcohol, acetone, methyl ethyl ketone: flush down sewer drain
Solvents, non-chlorinated (water-soluble)	Mineral spirits, paint or lacquer thinners: pour into absorbent material, let fumes evaporate, dispose of in trash

WARNING: If a cleaning product contains solvents, or has label warnings such as "flammable" or "poison," check with local authorities for instructions.

NOTE: Hazardous wastes such as acids, oils, fuels, pesticides, and oil-based paints and solvents should be recycled where possible or taken to hazardous waste sites if available.

10
Indoor
Air Quality

On the question of how to improve our environment, air quality is one more area where our emphasis may be misplaced. Congress has just passed a new Clean Air act, the first in a decade or more. The act mandates less pollution from cars, better emission controls for industry, and elimination of acid rain. At the same time, and partly due to past government urging to make our houses more energy efficient, *indoor* air quality is getting worse.

Over the past four decades, we have used an increasing number of potentially dangerous chemical products in the home. Chemical pesticides, home care products, aerosol paints, solvents, air fresheners, and auxiliary heating products have all become a "natural" part of our lives.

At the same time we have improved caulks, weatherstripping, insulation, and window and door construction to the point that air exchange is greatly reduced, and therein lies the problem.

You may have read how an engineer in Los Angeles wore a pollution monitoring device on his belt, to measure smog levels in the city. When he returned home that evening he forgot to remove the monitor and wore it in his house for a time. When he remembered to remove the device he was amazed to find that the air inside his house was nearly twenty times as polluted as the outdoor air. Once again, the home has proven to be the least safe place you can be.

SOURCES OF INDOOR AIR POLLUTION

What are the sources of this air pollution, and how can we improve the air quality in our homes? Again, the way to reduce the consequences of using a product is to avoid using that product. If you cannot avoid using the product, then be sure you are not overusing it. Follow label application directions for any chemical product you use in your house.

Look for non-toxic alternatives to products you now use. For cleaning products, the simplest alternatives are often the best. For example, use only soapy water to clean gold jewelry or dinnerware. Because gold does not tarnish you need not use any chemical cleaning product. Use equal parts of salt and flour, mixed with a bit of vinegar to make a paste, to clean brass hardware or fixtures. Mere baking soda and water will remove the tarnish from silver. You can make a non-toxic drain cleaner by mixing baking soda and vinegar, and the best air freshener is an open window.

Although we spend 90 percent of our lives indoors (at home and work), and although our indoor air may be as much as twenty times as toxic as outdoor air, we continue to direct most of our energy and resources to cleaning up outdoor air. The chances are very good that, if you suffer an illness from poor air quality, your downfall has been the air inside your home or workplace. We'll look at a number of things you can do to improve the quality of the air inside your home, ranging from "precycling" to installing active air cleaners.

BE AN AIR POLLUTION DETECTIVE

Indoor air pollution can be the result of radon entry, unvented gas ranges or ovens, kerosene-fired supplementary heaters, attached garages, oil- or coal-fired furnaces, wood-burning stoves or fireplaces, and tobacco smoke.

Products of combustion that can endanger your health include carbon monoxide, nitrogen oxide, hydrocarbons, lead, sulphur dioxide, formaldehyde, and related compounds. Experts point out that most studies that estimate "safe" levels of these pollutants do not take into account the possible synergistic effects of combining two or more of these chemicals in the same space. Another criticism of "safe" level studies is that they may list a level that is safe for perfectly healthy people, without taking into consideration the fact that the same home may include family members who are young and healthy, cardiac patients, those who suffer from respiratory ailments and/or allergies, the chemically sensitive, pregnant women and their fetuses, and the elderly and injured. It is an obvious and accepted fact that tolerable levels of chemical toxicity vary greatly among the very young, very old, and those with allergies or high chemical sensitivities. Thus, we should not assume that, because most family members seem well, one or more might be exhibiting the symptoms of flu, rather than attributing the symptoms to poisoning from polluted air.

The symptoms to watch for, if you suspect indoor air pollution, are: headache, nausea, skin rash, drowsiness, difficulty in concentrating, and other flu-like symptoms. These symptoms may indicate the presence of high levels of carbon monoxide or formaldehyde, for example. If any member of your family exhibits one or more of these symptoms, and the symptoms are acute or long-lasting, consult your physician. If indoor air quality is the suspect, ask your doctor or local health officials to recommend an industrial hygienist. A hygienist can use various testing devices to check home air pollution levels.

There may be non-physical symptoms of indoor air problems. For example, an unusual problem with fogged window glass may point to burn-through of the heat exchanger on your furnace. Moisture is given off during the combustion process when gas is burned. If there is a leak in the heat exchanger, the moisture can be released into the house, rather than going up the furnace chimney. Gases such as carbon monoxide also are released into the house. If window glass that normally shows no condensation suddenly (in heating season) fogs over, have your furnace heat exchanger checked. Also, have a professional check the burner efficiency of your furnace before each heating season. Symptoms of poor air/fuel mix or poor burner adjustment include a "dancing" flame or one that is very yellow or orange, not blue.

CARBON MONOXIDE

Because it can be fatal within only a short period of time, you should be especially alert to the possibilities of carbon monoxide poisoning. Burning carbon products such as gas, wood, oil, coal, or charcoal release carbon monoxide. Poisoning from carbon monoxide obviously occurs most often during the winter heating season, but may occur any time because of vent failure or from running a car in an attached garage. Faulty gas-burning furnaces plus poor ventilation are a sure recipe for disaster with carbon monoxide poisoning.

Carbon monoxide will replace oxygen in the blood supply, and in any room with equal proportions of carbon monoxide and oxygen the carbon monoxide will be absorbed in the bloodstream much more readily. If you suspect that someone is the victim of carbon monoxide poisoning, call 911 or a medical emergency team, because emergency services are equipped with pure oxygen, which will cleanse the system of carbon monoxide much more quickly than simply breathing ordinary room or outdoor air.

The car is a primary culprit in carbon monoxide poisoning. Running the car in an attached garage to warm it up in cold weather or running it while the car is stuck in snow can direct gas from leaking mufflers directly into the car and prove fatal to the occupants.

RADON

Radon is a radioactive gas that cannot be detected by the senses because it is odorless, colorless, and tasteless. Back in the 1960s, radon was identified when houses were built with materials that had been contaminated by uranium mine wastes. Radon is suspected of being second only to tobacco smoking as a cause of lung cancer. The Environmental Protection Agency estimates that radon may cause 100 lung cancer deaths per day.

A curie is a measurement of radioactivity; a picocurie is one-trillionth of a curie, and it is the unit used to measure the presence of radon. The permissible limits for radon are set at 4 picocuries per liter of air, or 4pCi/1. Inexpensive tests are available so you can test your home for radon.

Testing for Presence of Radon

Charcoal test canisters, available at home centers and department stores, offer an inexpensive test method to homeowners. The test, including laboratory work, costs about $20. To use the unit you simply remove the lid and set the container of activated charcoal in a suspect area, usually a base-

ment if your home has one, or in a laundry room. Let the unit sit for three to seven days, then replace the lid and send it off to the laboratory.

A more sophisticated test device is called the alpha track unit, which uses a sheet of polycarbonate plastic as a recording surface. The plastic sheet is left in place for three to six months. The exposed plastic sheet is struck by alpha particles from decaying radon, and the resulting "dents" in the plastic are counted by a laboratory to determine the level of radon present. These alpha track tests cost between $25 and $50 each and include the price of the laboratory work.

If these home tests show no radon, or show radon levels within the permissible 4pCi/1 range, your home is safe to occupy. You may decide to retest periodically, because radon levels may change with other conditions. For example, recent tests show an increase in some basement radon levels during periods of heavy rainfall.

Controlling Radon

Recommended steps for radon control include sealing basement cracks with caulk or with hydraulic cement if water is leaking in the crack. After sealing all cracks, apply a coat of waterproofing sealer such as United Gypsum Laboratories' Drylok to any bare concrete (or concrete block) basement walls.

Have a heating contractor install ducts to bring in outside combustion air for your furnace or fireplace. Using indoor air for combustion creates a negative pressure in the house, and negative pressure can cause radon to leak into the basement.

Provide plenty of ventilation to the entire basement to improve air quality. It is especially important that shop areas and attached garages be well ventilated, to prevent buildup of fumes from shop chemicals or carbon dioxide or gasoline fumes from the garage.

STATE — EPA REGION

Alabama — 4	Kentucky — 4	North Dakota — 8
Alaska — 10	Louisiana — 6	Ohio — 5
Arizona — 9	Maine — 1	Oklahoma — 6
Arkansas — 6	Maryland — 3	Oregon — 10
California — 9	Massachusetts — 1	Pennsylvania — 3
Colorado — 8	Michigan — 5	Rhode Island — 1
Connecticut — 1	Minnesota — 5	South Carolina — 4
Delaware — 3	Mississippi — 4	South Dakota — 8
District of Columbia — 3	Missouri — 7	Tennessee — 4
Florida — 4	Montana — 8	Texas — 6
Georgia — 4	Nebraska — 7	Utah — 8
Hawaii — 9	Nevada — 9	Vermont — 1
Idaho — 10	New Hampshire — 1	Virginia — 3
Illinois — 5	New Jersey — 2	Washington — 10
Indiana — 5	New Mexico — 6	West Virginia — 3
Iowa — 7	New York — 2	Wisconsin — 5
Kansas — 7	North Carolina — 4	Wyoming — 8

EPA REGIONAL OFFICES

EPA Region 1
Room 2203
JFK Federal Building
Boston, MA 02203
(617) 223-4845

EPA Region 2
26 Federal Plaza
New York, NY 10278
(212) 264-2515

EPA Region 3
841 Chestnut Street
Philadelphia, PA 19107
(215) 597-8320

EPA Region 5
230 South Dearborn Street
Chicago, IL 60604
(312) 353-2205

EPA Region 6
1445 Ross Avenue
Dallas, TX 75202-2733
(214) 655-7208

EPA Region 7
726 Minnesota Avenue
Kansas City, KS 66101
(913) 236-2803

EPA Region 4
345 Courtland Street, NE
Atlanta, GA 30365
(404) 881-3776

EPA Region 8
Suite 1300
One Denver Place
999 18th Street
Denver, CO 80202
(303) 283-1710

EPA Region 9
215 Fremont Street
San Francisco, CA 94105
(415) 974-8076

EPA Region 10
1200 Sixth Avenue
Seattle, WA 98101
(206) 442-7660

If you do detect high levels of radon, don't panic. Take enough time to find an experienced contractor who will assess the severity of the problem and plan how to deal with it. Don't let yourself be stampeded into spending thousands of dollars to correct the radon problem. For example, one house in New Jersey had a radon level of 3500 pCi/1. Using good ventilation techniques, a contractor reduced the radon level to only 2 pCi/1, at a cost of $1,300 to the homeowner.

If you need further advice on a radon problem, most states now have radiation protection offices to help you. Or check with your local building department or a building inspector for advice. You may be able to get help by calling your regional Environmental Protection Agency (EPA) office.

MATERIALS AND FURNISHINGS

Some time ago the workers in some newly-remodeled offices began to exhibit flu-like symptoms when exposed to the new paneling, office partitions, acoustic materials, paint, and carpeting. The employer immediately began to conduct a study on the source of the employee illnesses, because the offices belonged to the Environmental Protection Agency. At last report it seems that no single culprit is the source of the problem, but the obvious lesson is that we should be sure to provide adequate or even forced ventilation when introducing building products into our homes.

As mentioned elsewhere, we should let new building products "air out" outdoors, before moving them inside for installation. This advice goes for new paneling, carpeting, cabinets, and other components. When the products are installed, leave the windows open and run fans until the "new smell" is gone. Avoid using solvent or oil-based paints, to eliminate the solvent fumes from your living area. Use latex paints, and plan your painting during spring or summer, when heating equipment is not running and you can leave doors and windows open for good ventilation.

If you or your co-workers feel any symptoms in the workplace, ask managers for a check of air quality. If you are a manager, remember that work quality and production levels suffer when workers are affected by poor air quality.

HOUSEHOLD PRODUCTS

In Chapter 9, "Hazardous Waste," we discussed the need to eliminate household products that could be a danger to the environment. Keep in mind that many of these product threats are multi-dimensional, because they affect personal health and air quality in addition to damaging the general environment.

Products that contain chlorine are a prime example. Floor care products such as wax removers and paint strippers may contain some form of chlorine. If the fumes from these products are permitted to enter the combustion chamber on a forced air furnace they can form hydrochloric acid, which is highly corrosive. The effect can be the destruction of your heat exchanger, which in turn will permit harmful gases such as carbon monoxide to enter your home. How serious is this threat, really?

I once received a call from a reader (at *Family Handyman* magazine) who had lost three furnaces in a matter of months. My first question to him was: Do you strip and refinish furniture in your basement shop? He was astounded at my question, because he had not thought to suspect the paint strippers in the case of the furnace failures. Neither had the furnace installer guessed the problem: he just kept replacing those furnaces, never suspecting the source. Yet my local gas company's experts state that they have seen many cases of acid damage to furnaces, when paint strippers were used frequently. Might we conclude that the warnings to "use with adequate ventilation" are a bit understated? Refer to Chapter 9 for a more detailed discussion of eliminating pesticides, household care products, and other air-polluters from your home.

HEATING EQUIPMENT

During the oil shortage of the 1970s, there was a great movement to get back to basics, namely heating with wood. The magazine I worked for even did a book on the subject of how to cut, split, and store wood for home consumption. It soon became apparent that this "natural" energy source could be a major polluter, when used over a wide area. Aside from the obvious drawbacks of cutting and carrying wood in, then carrying the ashes out, both indoor and outdoor air quality suffered from the experiment. Everyone loves the smell of a wood fire, and a fireplace can be a romantic setting, but the truth is that they are hazardous to indoor air quality if they are not handled properly. After the increase in popularity of wood-burning equipment, doctors reported an increase in respiratory illnesses, especially among children of families who burned wood. If you are considering buying wood-burning equipment, make sure that the heater (stove or fireplace) is well built and properly installed. Have your fireplace ducted to bring in outside air for combustion, and keep a glass door in place to prevent smoke buildup inside the house. The door will also prevent the fireplace from exhausting conditioned air outside during combustion.

Kerosene Heaters

Another blunder of the 1970s was the introduction of unvented kerosene heaters for primary or auxiliary heating in living areas. I have used kerosene heaters in the workplace for years with no obvious problems, but this was in buildings that were under construction and therefore leaking fresh air into the space. I also remember the night my family would have died from carbon monoxide

poisoning, had my mother not awakened with a terrible headache. That was on a cold Missouri night when my parents had decided to leave a kerosene cookstove burning for extra heat. The worst that happened was that the family stood outside, wrapped in blankets and shivering under the clearest sky I will ever remember, while my mother and father aired out the house to remove the fumes. I need not express my own opinion on whether it is safe to use such heaters unvented. I would *never* use any such heater inside, if it were unvented. I know that the manufacturers contend that it is safe to operate such heaters without venting, but I would never do it or advise anyone else to do it. There can be no combustion without combustion gases, and I want those gases vented outside.

Furnaces

Have your furnace or boiler checked by a service technician each season, particularly if the heating equipment is more than five years old. In addition to inspecting the burner for proper adjustment — an important point for indoor air quality — the service technician can use inspector's mirrors, long-handled devices with the mirror heads set at an angle, to look up into the burner and heat exchanger to be sure they are not rusted or burnt through.

COOKSTOVES

You may have noticed that kitchen gas cooktops, stoves, and ovens are the only unvented combustion appliances in your house. Did you ever wonder why these burners are not required to be vented? The theory was that, while furnaces and water heaters must have direct vents, cooking appliances would be exempted because they are used only occasionally, and usually for short periods of time. While that may have been true in the past, today's weatherproofing requirements make gas cooking appliances suspect as indoor polluters. Combine today's super-tight houses with the four or five hours it takes to cook a Thanksgiving turkey, and you will see that there is a potential problem.

Most gas cooking appliances today have exhaust hoods for venting odors and combustion products. The problem may be that, unless you manually activate the exhaust hood's blower motor, you will have no ventilation. If using the cooking equipment for any extended time period, always turn on the vent hood blower to ensure that combustion products are safely exhausted. On days when temperatures are not severely cold, there is still no substitute for opening doors and windows to air out the space completely.

ASBESTOS

Asbestos came to the public's attention when long-term asbestos workers began to develop lung cancer and other respiratory health problems. Most of those afflicted worked for companies that made building products that contained asbestos. These products included insulation, floor tiles, ceiling tiles, wallboard taping compounds, pipe insulation, and brake shoes for cars. The asbestosis and other diseases resulted only after long years of daily or regular asbestos exposure. Most people will never contact enough asbestos fibers to cause health worries, because asbestos is now banned from use in most products.

The danger from asbestos is from breathing airborne asbestos particles, and in most cases asbestos is in a static condition, so it is not a cause for worry. Even if you have a lot of asbestos in your house, such as insulated hot water pipes in an older boiler/radiator system, do not worry. Most consumer reports assure you that asbestos that is not damaged is safe. The Environmental Protection Agency, in their booklet "Report to Congress on Indoor Air Quality," tells of a field study com-

paring airborne outdoor asbestos levels with prevailing indoor levels in forty-three federal buildings with asbestos materials. The EPA report states: "An interim report . . . indicates no statistical difference between indoor and outdoor levels [of asbestos], even in buildings with damaged asbestos-containing materials." Not only is there no concern for homeowners from breathing asbestos, it is likely that removing asbestos-containing from schools and other public buildings may be a waste of time and money.

TOBACCO SMOKE

While the nation invests heavily in research to find a cure for cancer, health officials estimate that fully one-third of all cancers could be prevented if we would all stop smoking. It is further estimated that the economic impact of indoor air pollution runs into the *tens of billions* of dollars annually. These billions of lost dollars are the result of lost earnings due to sickness, direct medical costs, and lower productivity while on the job.

While burning wood has been shown to increase directly the incidence of respiratory illness, most medical experts agree that the worst problem for an infant is to have a mother who smokes.

Listen to the words of the EPA bulletin, "Report to Congress on Indoor Air Quality," page 11: "Published reports of the Surgeon General and the National Research Council (NRC) of the National Academy of Sciences conclude that exposure to environmental tobacco smoke (ETS) [passive smoking] is a cause of lung cancer in healthy non-smokers and is responsible for both acute and chronic respiratory and other health impacts in sensitive populations, including children of smokers. Published risk estimates place ETS among the most harmful indoor pollutants, and higher in risk than many environmental pollutants currently regulated by EPA." The study goes on to say: "EPA total exposure monitoring studies

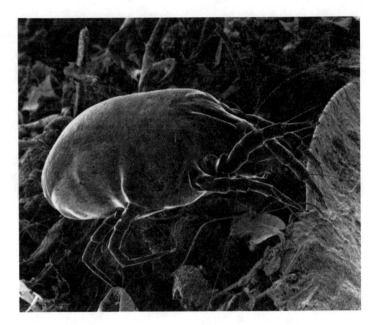

Microscopic dust mites and their excretions are too small to be filtered out by "dust-stop" furnace filters and can cause many family allergies. Photo courtesy of Honeywell Inc.

have shown that ETS is the dominant source of particulate matter in buildings where smoking is allowed, and that ETS contributes a significant fraction of carbon monoxide and volatile organic compounds (VOCs) — including benzene — exposures. Health studies by EPA's Health Effects Research Lab show that ETS contributes the bulk of mutagenic activity in indoor air."

DUST MITES

A major contributor to allergies, the dust mite is a microscopic house guest that looks like a cross between a spider and a crab. Dust mites nestle in such cozy places as bedding and carpets. You'll probably never see one, because a very large dust mite might measure 60 microns in size. The eye of a needle is 760 microns, so you could fit about thirteen fat dust mites into a needle's eye. There may be as many as two million of these handsome rascals in your bed: they feed on human skin flakes, or dander. Each person sheds thousands of these skin flakes each day, so the mites don't lack for food.

The dust mite's fecal pellets cause allergic reactions when they are inhaled. The mites themselves dry out, and their skeletons float on air when the mites die, adding to the other allergens in the air.

How can you control these pesky critters? The Asthma and Allergy Foundation of America recommends that you:

1. Vacuum upholstered furniture weekly.

2. Cover new mattresses and pillows with a zippered, dustproof cover.

3. Remove bedroom carpeting in rooms occupied by highly sensitive people.

4. Wash bedding in water that is 130°F or hotter.

5. Increase home ventilation and reduce humidity.

6. Air-condition in hot weather.

7. Install a high efficiency air cleaner to remove the mites' fecal pellets and other irritants.

IMPROVING INDOOR AIR QUALITY

House Plants

It has long been recognized that we could solve many of our air pollution problems if we would plant enough trees. The trees consume carbon dioxide and give off oxygen in return. In his book on the Middle East, *The Source*, James Michener has one character asking another which nation would ultimately win the struggle for national supremacy. "Germany" was the answer. Why? "Because they plant trees."

The same is true of indoor air quality: plant activity will cleanse the air. How many plants would it take to do the job? NASA estimates that if we would have one plant, 10 to 12 inches in diameter, for each 100 square feet of floor space, we could greatly reduce indoor air pollution. The best plant choices for improving air quality include chrysanthemum, Chinese evergreen, spider plant, philodendron, peace lily, mother-in-law's tongue, and English ivy. The plant approach is an inexpensive and attractive way to brighten up the house's interior while improving air quality. However, you must water house plants with care, because overwatering can encourage mold and mildew growth. The mold and mildew spores can then contribute to indoor air pollution. Plant your house plants in plastic pots rather than clay pots. Clay pots retain moisture and encourage mildew and mold. Then water the plants sparingly.

AIR-TO-AIR HEAT EXCHANGERS

If your home is very humid, or you have allergies, or you feel the house is so tight that air quality is suffering, you can have installed in your home a device called a heat exchanger. This is not a do-it-yourself job: the heat exchanger employs a system of ductwork to carry stale air outside, bring fresh air inside, and do so in a manner permitting the heat from outgoing air to be transferred to the incoming fresh air, so the air is changed without losing the heat you have paid for.

Obviously, one difficult problem is how to conceal these added ducts, if the system is being installed as a retrofit in an existing house. The professional installer can solve this problem by routing the ducts between existing floor or ceiling joists, or he may have to install drop ceilings or soffits to conceal the new ducts. This is not work for an amateur, because a poor duct plan could cut up the interior and reduce the appeal of the house.

The pro to seek out, if you want to explore a heat exchanger installation, is a heating, ventilating, and air conditioning (HVAC) contractor. The contractor is trained to calculate and determine which heat exchanger unit is best for your job, what sort of blower must be used, duct size, and other questions of air movement and air volume capacity. Look for this expert in the Yellow Pages under "Heating Contractors." Make sure the contractor is licensed, bonded, and insured, and check his references.

KEEP EQUIPMENT CLEAN

In the discussion of energy in Chapter 12, we will cover the need to keep the furnace, ducts, and air conditioning equipment clean and properly adjusted. This advice is important for good energy efficiency, but it is also important when trying to maintain indoor air quality. A forced air furnace or air conditioner can become nothing more than a dust machine, blowing dirt, pollen, mildew spores, and other pollutants through the house in an unbroken cycle, if filters are neglected.

Replace furnace filters monthly when the blower motor is moving conditioned air, whether heated or cooled. Have furnace air ducts cleaned frequently (follow your service technician's advice) and remove and clean the air registers at least

Microscopic bacteria and mold spores contribute to allergies. They can be controlled through good air filtration and by venting excess moisture. Photo courtesy of Honeywell Inc.

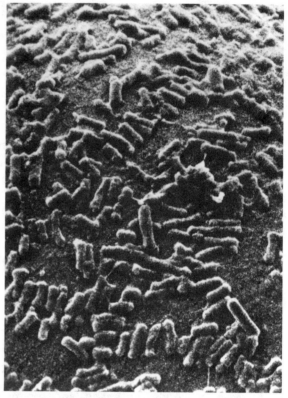

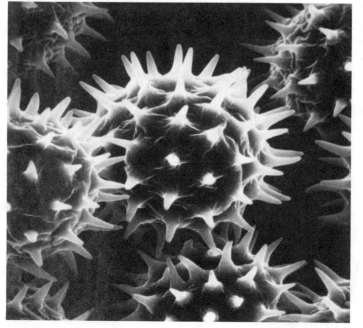

This is what pollen looks like under a microscope. An estimated 70 million people suffer from allergies caused by these and other airborne pollutants. Photo courtesy of Honeywell Inc.

An electronic air filter can be installed in your furnace's cold air return duct to improve indoor air quality. Photo courtesy of Honeywell Inc.

twice a year. Have the furnace burner cleaned and adjusted before the start of each heating season, to be sure that the burner is achieving a clean, efficient burn.

AIR CONDITIONERS

If you have central air conditioning, you have an A-shaped cooling coil above the forced air furnace. The cooling coils contain Freon®, which cools the coils. Then air is blown across the cooling coils, cooled, and distributed through the house by the furnace blower motor.

As the air is blown over the cooling coils, any dust, dirt, pollen, lint, grease, or smoke in the air is attracted to the cooling coils like a magnet. The pollutants quickly coat the coils, forming a layer of dirt that insulates the coils and reduces their cooling capacity. Because the cooling efficiency is reduced, the unit uses more energy to meet the demands of the thermostat. In addition, bacteria and fungus breed in the dirt and can cause air quality problems. Such bacterial or fungus growth can cause problems like the Legionnaire's disease, named for the illness that afflicted American Legion members who were attending a hotel convention.

The only filter on most home air conditioners is the fiberglass and aluminum furnace filter, called a "dust-stop filter." These filters can trap lint, grease, and larger dirt or pollen particles. While

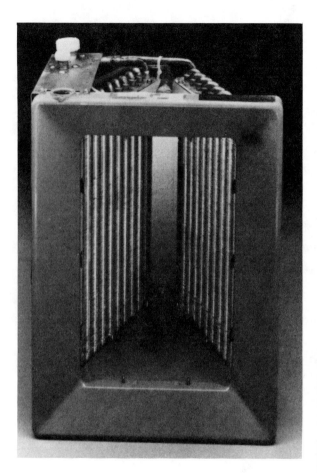

The cooling coils in your air conditioner can trap airborne dirt and lower the unit's efficiency. Keep cooling coils clean with an electronic air filter. Photos courtesy of Honeywell Inc.

dust-stop filters reduce the buildup of dirt on the coils, they do not filter out smoke, most pollens, viral matter, fungus or mildew spores, or dust mites and small dust particles. If your only filter is the ordinary dust-stop filter, have the coils professionally cleaned every four years.

Companies such as Honeywell Inc. make filters that are far more efficient than the dust-stop filters. Filters called media air filters are made of a filter paper that works in two ways: they screen out larger particles and trap smaller particles on the filter fibers, in much the same way that flies are trapped on flypaper.

The best filter is the electronic air cleaner, which is installed directly in the heating and cooling system, usually in the cold air return to replace the dust-stop filter. Electronic filters are made by a number of companies, among them Honeywell Inc. Honeywell reports that their electronic air cleaners will trap up to 95 percent of all airborne particles, which prevents the particles from fouling the cooling coils or from being recirculated through the home.

The best electronic air cleaners can be removed from the unit and washed in a sink or dishwasher when dirty. The filters operate on about the same electricity as used by a 40-watt bulb, and pay for themselves by improving the efficiency of the air conditioner and the quality of indoor air.

Window air conditioners have filters of fiberglass or plastic fiber. These filters should be removed and washed weekly during the cooling season. Use a vacuum cleaner with a brush attachment to clean the aluminum cooling fins, then use a sponge dampened with bleach to clean off mildew or mold that is on the conditioner unit or coils.

Electronic air cleaners cannot be fitted on window air conditioners, but you can have the superior electronic cleaning by using a portable unit.

"PERFECT CLIMATE"

If you are building a new home, check out Honeywell Inc.'s Perfect Climate™ Home. Honeywell, a long-time leader in residential temperature controls and air cleaning equipment, has helped develop a new concept in home comfort and cleanliness. There are five elements to the Perfect Climate™ house:

1. an electronic air cleaner;

2. a premium programmable thermostat;

3. optimum efficiency heating and cooling equipment;

4. proper ventilation and air distribution; and

5. humidity controls.

Estimated cost of this equipment runs between 1 and 2 percent of the cost of the house. Honeywell estimates that their electronic air cleaners will pay for themselves in about five years, while their top-of-the-line programmable thermostats may have a payback of only one year.

Honeywell maintains that indoor "weather" affects family comfort; energy savings; health, both physical and mental; and heating and cooling costs. Furthermore, because we spend up to 90 percent of our time indoors, and because we can control our indoor environment with today's technology, we can have improved health, comfort, and safety with the ultimate in convenience and reliability. What follows is a review of the five components of the Perfect Climate™ Home and the advantages of each component.

Electronic Air Cleaner

According to the Environmental Protection Agency (EPA) the most polluted air you breathe is indoors, most often in your own home. Indoor air

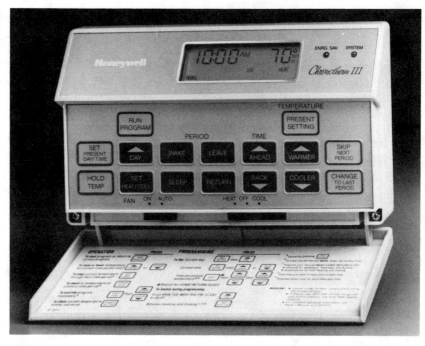

High quality thermostats can maintain indoor temperatures within a range of 2 degrees or less. Photo courtesy of Honeywell Inc.

can reach pollution levels twenty times as high as outdoor air. Pollutants trapped in this enclosed environment can build to dangerously high levels, and this buildup is complicated by the synergistic effects of multiple pollutants.

An estimated 99 percent of indoor pollutants are microscopic particles that are invisible to the human eye. Ordinary furnace dust-stop filters do not trap particles smaller than 100 microns in size, so these particles are continuously being recirculated throughout the house. Improved media filters can trap particles as small as 0.5 microns, meaning that media filters are ten times as effective as dust-stop filters.

Electronic air cleaners electrostatically trap particles as small as .01 micron, which means they remove up to 95 percent of all airborne particles. Particles this small include pollen, plant and mildew spores, dust, cooking or tobacco smoke, insecticide dusts, bacteria, and some viruses.

Programmable Thermostat

The human body may feel even slight 2 degree temperature variations and become uncomfortable at any greater temperature swing. Honeywell's Chronotherm III will maintain a temperature within one degree of the temperature selected.

Efficient Heating and Cooling Equipment

Honeywell's system insists on using high-efficiency heating and cooling equipment. By definition, a gas furnace is high-efficiency if it has an Annual Fuel Utilization Efficiency (AFUE, shown on the furnace label) of 80 or more percent. Any air conditioner or heat pump is rated high-efficiency if it has a Seasonal Energy Efficiency Ratio (SEER, again listed on the product label) higher than 10. Older equipment has no such rating because the equipment was not required to carry such information; the common efficiency of furnaces more than ten years old was about 65 percent.

Ventilation and Air Distribution

The air delivery systems in the house should be balanced to provide maximum comfort to the occupants and peak energy efficiency. The air should be clean and humidified and should be delivered in proper quantities for comfort. New, tightly built homes may require an outdoor source of ventilation. Poorly ventilated houses may trap airborne pollutants or gases inside the house, may have air that is stratified in alternate cold and warm layers, and may be drafty and uncomfortable.

Humidity Controls

Controlling humidity levels is the last component of the Perfect Climate™ system. A person feels as comfortable when the relative humidity is at 30 and the temperature is at 70°F, as when the relative humidity is only 20 and the air temperature is an inefficient 80°F. Note that we are not saying you will be *warmer*, but that you will be *more comfortable* at the lower temperature and higher relative humidity. Depending on outdoor weather, the ideal indoor humidity will vary between 30 and 60 percent.

Controlling the indoor humidity will slow the growth of bacteria and viruses that can cause colds and allergies, and will reduce dry throats and nasal passages during heating season. Proper humidity levels can also protect furniture and the house interior trim from drying out, shrinking, and cracking. Too little humidity in the house will also cause clothes to cling and produce annoying static shock.

Also included in the Perfect Climate™ is a radon monitor that provides a constant check on indoor radon levels. Located in the lower level of the house (radon gases enter most often through the soil), this constant monitoring permits a radon ventilation system to be activated in the event that radon levels rise above 4 pCi/1.

Honeywell points out that such pollutants as radon and microscopic dust mites were undiscov-

ered until the 1960s, and the mandate for tighter house construction has meant that houses trap pollutants that were formerly exhausted. It is estimated that we have gone from one air exchange per hour, in older, drafty houses, down to one air exchange in ten hours with modern construction. Given the increase in chemical products that are used in the home, there is sure to be an ongoing battle to improve indoor air quality.

SMART HOUSE

The housing industry made history in the spring of 1990 by breaking ground for the all-electric SMART HOUSE. The project, conceived in the early 1980s by the National Association of Home Builders, is located in a project called Southland, just east of Atlanta, Georgia. The house, managed by the Edison Electric Institute, combines all the latest electronic technology with the most energy-efficient thermal wrap now possible, meaning that the exterior envelope of the house is now a super-insulated cocoon. The SMART HOUSE will provide the highest energy efficiency, home safety, and the most comfortable indoor environment possible.

A highly efficient, variable-speed Carrier Hydro-tech 2000 heat pump provides climate control and water heating. A dual electric oven combines both microwave and convection cooking capabilities for the best energy conservation plus versatility.

Because there is no combustion for either heating or cooking, there are no combustion gases to pollute indoor air or to require venting. There are no holes in walls or roofs for chimneys or vents, so the insulation or thermal blanket is not interrupted and no conditioned air goes up a chimney. All hot water piping and air ducts are insulated because energy conservation is best when heat is delivered only where needed, with precise control.

The thermal envelope of the SMART HOUSE

also includes double-pane windows with low-emissivity (Low-E) glass, and exterior doors are insulated. This attention to all details recognizes the "weak link" reality of heat loss: heat will flow to cold by any avenue possible, so in a well-constructed home any weak link in the conservation chain will be the avenue of greatest energy loss.

To avoid the cost of building an ever-increasing number of electrical power plants, utility companies offer discounts for energy used during off-peak hours. Most family activities in the home peak in the early morning and during the dinner hour. In the SMART HOUSE a communication processor called an Electric Utility Gateway Device will link the occupants with the utility company. The system permits you to program energy use to occur during off-peak hours, at lower costs for the power. For example, you might place wash-ed clothes in the dryer and program the dryer to go on while you sleep, when power demand is low.

The familiar electrical service in a house will be replaced by a network of coaxial cables that will carry all of the electrically-powered house services. Convenience Centers will replace electrical outlets, and you can plug in and operate telephones, stereos and other appliances, and receive cable TV or roof antenna signals at any Convenience Center. Another departure is that power will not flow to the Centers until there is a demand for it. Electronic chips activate the system when occupants plug recognized appliances into the Convenience Centers, creating a Closed Loop System that prevents any shocks or fires from accidental contact. A device that will replace the ordinary light switch will act as a zoned room thermostat, operate various house alarms, as well as turning on any light or any combination of lights.

Under today's electrical codes, electrical outlets that are near any water source must have a Ground Fault Circuit Interrupter (GFCI) to prevent dangerous shocks. In the SMART HOUSE, all electrical outlets, whether 120 or 240 volts, will have GFCI protection. Any shorted or otherwise faulty appliance will block power to the Center the moment it is plugged in.

Looking beyond, into the next decade and the next century, the technology used in the SMART HOUSE will expand to be a force in energy conservation and in environmental protection. The concept should reduce the need for more electrical generating plants and help reduce air pollution. It will provide a cleaner indoor environment by eliminating combustion of fossil fuels from the home. Manufacturers of home appliances already are researching and developing new products that will no doubt revolutionize the way we live.

CHECKLIST

INDOOR AIR QUALITY

❏ Have the furnace burner cleaned and adjusted each fall.

❏ To prevent carbon monoxide poisoning, do not warm up the car engine in an attached garage.

❏ Buy a radon charcoal test kit for about $20 and check for radon.

❏ Let new building materials "air out" outdoors before installing them in the house. Provide good ventilation until the "new smell" is gone from products.

❏ Provide extra ventilation in any area in which you follow hobbies that require any chemicals, such as model building, woodworking, photographic processing, pottery, or painting.

❏ Gas appliances such as stoves, cooktops, and ovens can give off dangerous combustion gases. Be sure all burners and standing pilot lights are well cleaned and adjusted. Gas flames should be blue, not yellow or orange.

❏ Asbestos is dangerous only if fibers become airborne. Do not disturb asbestos insulation or products that contain asbestos. If remodeling, have the asbestos removal and disposal done by a professional.

❏ Tobacco is one of the chief indoor air pollutants. Don't smoke indoors and do ask visitors to refrain from smoking.

❏ House plants can help cleanse the indoor air. NASA recommends one 10- to 12-inch (diameter) plant for each 100 square feet of floor space.

❏ Maintain indoor humidity levels between 30 and 60 percent relative. Too much moisture can cause mildew, mold, bacteria, and musty odors. These in turn can aggravate allergies.

❏ Use kitchen or bath exhaust vents when cooking or bathing. Exhaust vents remove odors, smoke, and grease in addition to removing excess humidity.

❏ Most indoor humidity problems occur in summer. If your house is too humid in winter and summer, have a heating contractor install a heat recovery ventilator.

❏ If indoor humidity is too low, install a humidifier in your heating/cooling system.

❏ Install an electronic air cleaner to replace your dust-stop furnace filter. Electronic air cleaners can remove up to 95 percent of air particles including those as small as 0.01 micron.

❏ Save owner's manuals from furnaces, air conditioners, and other gas appliances. Have the units cleaned and adjusted at periods suggested by your owner's manual. Have air ducts cleaned and clean or replace filter elements before they become clogged and inefficient.

11
Business Recycling

My county government (Hennepin County in Minnesota) estimates that about 55 percent of the waste generated in this county is from businesses, and that 50 percent of that business total consists of such easily recyclable materials as paper and cardboard.

The county further estimates that the amount of waste generated per employee is 3.21 pounds (commercially) and 8.16 pounds in the industrial sector per day. The average office employee will generate .67 pounds of high-grade office paper and .65 pounds of mixed-grade paper per day. *Fortune* magazine has estimated that the annual amount of office-generated waste paper would make a wall 12 feet high that would stretch from New York City to Los Angeles. From these figures it can be seen that our workplaces must take a leading role in reducing the waste stream.

Hennepin County suggests that businesses can benefit in several ways by participating in an aggressive recycling program. First, your business can enhance its public image while doing its fair share to keep the environment clean. This cooperation will also help to ensure that we conserve natural resources so that the future of our businesses is secured. But the best reason, or the one that should automatically appeal to the prudent business person, is a reduction of overhead through reducing or eliminating disposal costs.

Examples for business savings abound. The municipal liquor store in Mound, Minnesota eliminated its waste hauling service altogether by recycling corrugated cardboard boxes, which comprised 95 percent of its total waste generation.

A huge office complex in suburban Minneapolis reduced its waste hauling costs by $5,000 in 1989. The complex accomplished this by recycling office paper and aluminum beverage cans: in an eight-month period it recycled 58 tons of waste.

How much can your business save by recycling? That depends on the size, type, and scope of your business, as well as the number of employees. My county estimates that an office complex having 3,000 employees might save nearly $11,000 per year in disposal costs. This would be accomplished by a 30 percent reduction in the amount (by weight) of waste generated, through recycling. A reduction in the amount of waste to be hauled would obviously reduce the frequency of needed pickups by the waste hauler.

Another example, that of a retail store with only twelve employees and obviously low levels of waste generation, might save close to $3,000 per year, again through reducing the tonnage of waste generated and thus the number of pickup stops needed for waste removal.

BUSINESS RECYCLING BY TYPE

What sort of waste does the average business generate? It depends on the type of business, as we stated. Manufacturing plants generate large quantities of scrap materials. Foundries and other heavy manufactories already sell their metallic scrap, which they generate by the ton. The publisher/printer that I formerly worked for generated boxcar loads of waste paper, which was shipped out in trainloads and used to create cellulose insulation, egg cartons, and recycled papers. If your company is organizing a new recycling program, consider these suggestions.

Government Offices

A first step in recycling is to insist that your government, at every level, sets the example. City, county, and state government office buildings generate huge amounts of paper waste and aluminum beverage cans. School districts and hospitals are other institutions that can be organized to recycle. Any building large enough to include a cafeteria should have marked containers so that customers can sort their own trash as they dispose of it, for easy recycling.

Commercial Offices

Office buildings generate the most valuable paper waste, because they consume high-grade papers. Correspondence and computer papers are good examples of high-grade papers. These are the most valuable papers and will bring the best salvage prices. These papers are known in the trade as "sorted white ledger." Other types of paper generated would be newsprint and corrugated cardboard shipping cartons. Ordinary paperboard products are not worth recycling and should be disposed of with other trash.

Shipping pallets have also come under scrutiny for possible recycling. There are now companies that rebuild damaged wood pallets to conserve wood. Other materials, such as more durable woods and fiberglass, are being used for building shipping pallets that will resist damage from forklift handling. Have your purchasing agent or plant engineer look into these savings, through either recycling or purchasing better products.

Hospitality Industry

Hospitality businesses such as restaurants and bars generate large quantities of glass containers and metal cans that hold food or beverages. In most instances, these glass or metal containers should be rinsed and sorted by type: glass containers by color, and metal containers by composition. The salvage value of aluminum containers at this writing is about 42 cents per pound, or about 1½ cents per can.

Waste food and garbage are handled by the usual sanitary disposal methods. Paper or paperboard food containers, any product that has come in contact with food, must be disposed of as garbage. Many cities now have waste-to-fuel incinerators that burn wastes to generate steam for electricity.

ORGANIZING FOR BUSINESS RECYCLING

If your business does not have a recycling plan, here is a procedural list proposed by my county government.

1. Assign an employee to organize and coordinate the effort.

2. Estimate the amount and type of waste that can be recycled.

3. Choose a method of collection, such as desktop containers, collection stations, or collection/sorting by custodian.

4. Investigate disposal options. Does your pre-

sent waste hauler accept sorted recyclables? Are optional recyclers offering pickup services? Are there drop points near your business or home?

5. Develop and implement company collection systems, and select a date to commence program.

6. Notify employees of the recycling policies and the date chosen for implementation.

Two points to keep in mind when considering your own business recycling plan are:

1. contact your city or county for free advice or help for implementing your plan; and

2. check with other businesses in the area to see how they are handling the problem. You may be able to avoid expensive mistakes by consulting with others who already have a program.

12
Conserving Home Energy

This book was conceived as one that would help conserve our natural resources while reducing the waste stream through recycling. However, perhaps no book that is concerned with conservation should ignore the subject of home energy. Certainly our consumption of energy in the home contributes directly to our waste and pollution problems. And, with a new energy crisis as well as mounting energy costs, perhaps we should review the subject of home energy.

Is there anything new that can be said about energy conservation? The subject received endless attention from our government and from the media during the crisis of the '70s. When fuel prices plateaued and other areas of the cost of living inflated, energy costs were relegated to the back burner. Still, there is some confusion evident on the subject, so a brief review might be helpful.

First of all, we are the victims of past building practices. Our building materials, methods, and codes were based on the assumption that we had an endless supply of cheap energy. It was simply cheaper to waste energy in massive amounts than to add more insulation, or build more efficient appliances, or install double-pane windows. To those who blame the building industry for this oversight, I ask: who would have paid a high price for an energy-efficient home in an era when monthly heating bills ranged between ten and twenty dollars? When the consumer is uncaring about cars

that get poor fuel mileage, or houses that waste energy by the bucket, there will be no momentum on the part of the industries to change.

With oil prices rising steeply, there is again concern on the part of the public. So, we will review some steps that consumers can take to reduce home fuel consumption.

UNDERSTANDING THERMAL EFFICIENCY

In my days as a magazine editor, at the height of our first oil crisis, we often wrote about how to reduce energy consumption. All the usual subjects — insulation, weatherstripping, double-pane windows, foam insulated doors — were covered. We often heard from some reader who lamented that he had spent hundreds of dollars on added attic insulation, and the fuel bills continued to climb. What was wrong?

Energy consumption in a home depends on three things. First, it depends on the efficiency of the furnace or air conditioner. Furnaces made before the energy crisis were manufactured to be about 65 percent efficient. That means they were built to waste 35 percent of the fuel. This waste was not meant to be a penalty: high stack (chimney) temperatures were maintained to be sure the exhaust

Courtesy of Lennox.

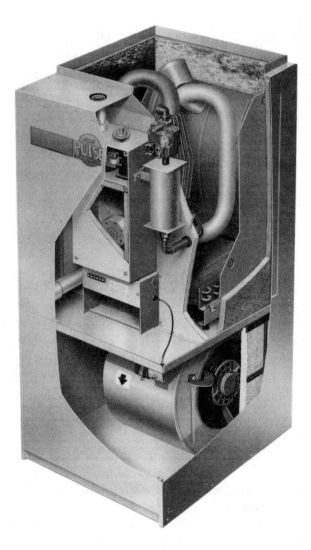

An example of new heating technology is seen in the Lennox Pulse furnace, which has an AFUE rating of 96.2. The Pulse combines spark plug ignition (no standing pilot light), outdoor combustion air, and intermittent ignition for high fuel efficiency. Courtesy of Lennox.

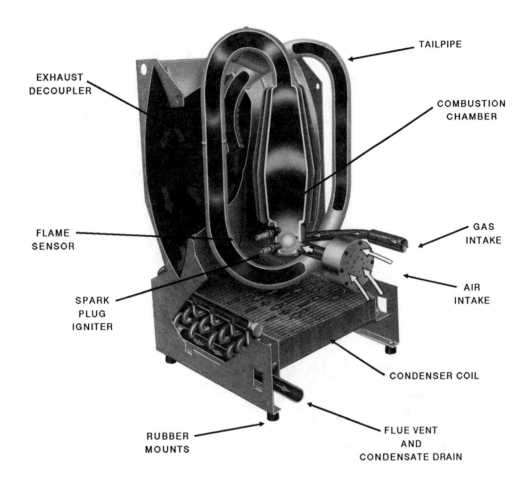

TAILPIPE

EXHAUST
DECOUPLER

COMBUSTION
CHAMBER

GAS
INTAKE

FLAME
SENSOR

AIR
INTAKE

SPARK
PLUG
IGNITER

CONDENSER COIL

RUBBER
MOUNTS

FLUE VENT
AND
CONDENSATE DRAIN

Courtesy of Lennox.

was hot enough to carry away all combustion gases, such as carbon monoxide. The efficiency rating was not, critical because the fuel was cheap, and was expected to stay cheap.

When fuel prices escalated, furnace and other heating appliance manufacturers engineered new technology into the units. Secondary heat exchangers and induced drafts were used to get the most possible energy out of every ounce of fuel. Furnace efficiencies were forced to 96 percent by these engineering changes.

The point of this information is that the first step for energy conservation must be an efficient heating plant. No matter how well you insulate, no matter how much money you spend on the thermal wrap (insulation, weatherstripping) you will still waste many dollars in fuel unless you install a more efficient heating appliance (forced air furnace or boiler). You can insulate to the maximum, and your old 65 percent efficiency furnace will still waste one of every three energy dollars you spend. If your furnace is more than ten years old, check (or have a service representative check) its efficiency levels. Anything that is less than 80 percent efficient is a likely candidate for replacement.

The second factor in home energy consumption is the thermal efficiency of the outer shell of the house. This factor includes the thickness and material content of all exterior walls; the thickness

If your home has average wall/ceiling insulation, 20 percent of your heat loss is through the basement walls. Build stud walls against basement walls and insulate. Photo courtesy of Owens-Corning.

Don't neglect to insulate the band joist area where the top of the concrete basement walls meets the band/floor joists. Photo courtesy of Owens-Corning.

Apply a 6-mil poly vapor barrier over the insulation, then finish with a layer of wallboard to prevent gas formation in case of fire reaching the fiberglass insulation. Photo courtesy of Owens-Corning.

and type of insulation blanket in walls and ceilings; the efficiency of windows and doors including double-pane glass and good weatherstripping; and the efficiency of the exterior doors. One might include ventilation here, because attic or ceiling space that is improperly vented encourages water vapor to be trapped and to condense in the insulation. Wet insulation is as useless on a cold day as wet socks. Be sure your attic ventilation is adequate.

The third factor in the equation, and one of the most important, is lifestyle. In the early '80s, a builder built many houses on the same plan: all were equipped and insulated alike. The builder offered to pay the heating bills of the family who was most conserving. The builder found to his amazement, when he checked all the utility bills, that wasteful families were spending about twice as much for heating as more conserving families. If you have children who leave doors and windows open, or play with the thermostat, or run in and out in cold weather, you will have high fuel bills.

On these three points — furnace efficiency, thermal efficiency, and lifestyle — we offer a few steps you should take to minimize energy consumption. Some steps may save little, when taken alone, but taking every step possible can result in combined savings that are really significant.

FURNACE EFFICIENCY

Under this heading we will include heating and air conditioning appliances of any kind. Conditioning inside air — whether you are heating or cooling it — is the largest consumer of energy. If you have an older, inefficient furnace or boiler, consider replacing it with a more efficient new unit. Forced air furnaces that have efficiency ratings of 90 percent or more can be bought at reasonable prices. Check the energy efficiency rating — EER — on any appliance you buy.

If you have a forced air furnace that is inefficient,

you must replace the whole unit. If you have an older boiler that fires steam or hot water heating you may be able to replace the old burner unit with a more efficient one. Check with your service representative to find what is possible to upgrade your particular unit.

If your furnace is rated with an efficiency of 80 percent or above, it will not pay to replace it for energy savings alone. You can, however, have the burner cleaned and adjusted to be sure the burner is working at peak efficiency. This is a job for a service representative, not for a homeowner.

Also, consider installing an energy-saving thermostat. These setback thermostats automatically reset the temperature so the house is comfortable while you are at home, but reduce temperature levels while you are away or while you sleep. If family members are home all day, the setback thermostat may not be worthwhile: just set the thermostat back a few degrees when you go to bed, and turn it up to more comfortable levels when you get up.

Insulate any hot water pipes or heating ducts. Your heating unit is most efficient when the heat (or cold) is delivered where it is needed. Clean and adjust burner units every season, and change the furnace filter every month during peak heating (or cooling, if you have central air) season.

If you have rooms that you do not use, do not shut the wall air registers. Any heat you send down the duct will be wasted if not used. Instead, shut off the damper in the duct, near the furnace, so no air will enter into the duct. Then shut the door to the room so heat from the rest of the house will not spill into the unused space.

Air Conditioning

The instructions given for the furnace apply equally to any attached central air conditioning. Installing clean filters and shutting duct dampers to unused rooms will reduce air conditioning costs.

The best return on your energy investment is to stop air loss. Caulk all cracks between non-moving materials, such as the crack between window trim and siding or stucco.

Check your home's exterior carefully. Though the cracks may seem to be caulked tight, cracks at the bottom of windows, around pipes or wires that penetrate the siding, and behind window shutters are often overlooked.

In addition, use a hose and nozzle to wash debris from the compressor cabinet that sits on a concrete slab outside.

Check your owner's manual: there may be oiling ports on the compressor blower motor that require periodic lubrication. (Some newer units may have sealed bearings that are permanently lubricated.)

Also, build a lattice or other sunscreen to shade the compressor unit of the air conditioner. Heat buildup from direct sunlight may make the unit work harder to cool the house.

THERMAL EFFICIENCY

The most crucial factor in the efficiency of the structure itself is the insulation blanket. If your attic or ceiling is accessible, by all means bring the insulation level of your attic up to your own local recommended levels. Your building department can tell you the right thickness of insulation for your area. Keep in mind, though, that the thickness of insulation recommended is purely a financial matter: how much insulation will pay for itself at today's energy prices. As energy prices rise, so does the recommended thickness of the insulation blanket.

We do not recommend trying to add "blow in" insulation to existing walls that already have some insulation. It is very difficult to get a uniform added thickness when there is existing insulation blocking the way. If there is some insulation in the walls, wait until you remodel or reside the house, and the wall cavities are accessible. Then fill the cavities with insulation, and/or install foam insulation board over the sheathing on the house exterior.

One point that is little understood, however, is that insulation efficiency depends on having a continuous blanket throughout the house. Having a proper insulation level in the ceiling will not stop insulation leaks in the walls.

The confusion arises because most of us think that hot air rises, which it does. But *heat* flows to cold, by nature's law; and it will flow in any direction, even down or sideways, to do so. Adding ceiling insulation increases heat loss through leaky walls: insulate the walls, and heat will escape through basement walls or floors.

Ideally, the insulation blanket should be continuous around the house perimeter. The key is to insulate any area that is accessible, such as the ceiling or attic, and upgrade wall insulation when you remodel or have an opportunity to do so.

CRACKS

There are two kinds of cracks in your house exterior, and both kinds will let conditioned air leak out. The first crack is between two materials or components that do not move. This can be a leak between a wood sill plate and the concrete foundation it rests on; or between house siding and a brick fireplace chimney; or a water pipe or electrical wire and the siding through which they penetrate; or the siding and the trim on a window or door. All these cracks — and any other cracks between non-moving materials that you can find on your house exterior — should be filled with caulk. Buy the best, longest-lasting caulk you can find, either acrylic latex or silicone caulk, and fill all cracks. To be sure the cracks are properly sealed, you should first remove any old caulk with a paint scraper or putty knife. Then apply the new caulk in a generous bead to completely seal the crack. Don't overlook the longest crack in your house: where the wood sill plate of the wall meets the concrete foundation or basement wall. And don't forget that the single most effective thing you can do, from a cost/return standpoint, is to seal all cracks with caulk or weatherstrip.

Which brings us to the second type of crack in your house: the crack between two components, at least one of which moves. These include cracks around doors and their frames, or between window sash and trim or stop. It is estimated that a crack 1/8 inch wide around a door or window can be the equivalent of a brick-size hole in the wall. If you have a dozen (or more) windows and two exterior doors that have leaking weatherstrip, it is easy to see that the net effective heat loss would be somewhat equal to removing an exterior door from its hinges.

Obviously, this supports our claim elsewhere that leaky windows and doors waste as much energy each year as the North Slope in Alaska can produce. There are any number of weatherstripping products available to those who wish to install it themselves, but it might be a good plan to hire a professional to dismantle and clean the windows, then install the very best weatherstripping available for your particular units.

When weatherstripping exterior doors, don't overlook the floor sweep or bottom weatherstrip. This seals the crack between the door bottom and threshold to prevent cold, dirt, and insects from entering. This is an often-overlooked area: I have inspected new homes that had no door sweeps to seal exterior door bottoms.

LIGHTING

Recent reports that I have seen estimate that Americans waste upwards of $20 billion per year in wasteful lighting products alone. While lighting is normally a small item in each household budget, it is nevertheless worthy of some consideration.

Small bulbs (in terms of wattage) use less energy than large bulbs. Fluorescent bulbs use less energy than incandescent bulbs, and may produce more light while doing so. New compact fluorescent bulbs that can replace incandescent bulbs in lamps or lighting fixtures use 18 watts, produce about 1100 lumens (light intensity equal to a 75-watt incandescent bulb), and last about 10,000 hours. A

bit pricey at around $18 per bulb, they will work for about half what the incandescent bulb will — about $30, compared to $60 for the incandescent — when compared over the lifetime of the fluorescent compact.

Consider your own lighting needs before you buy. Elderly people may need three times as much light as a young person, and proper light levels are especially important around stairs or other walking hazards. It is also important to maintain proper light levels in the kitchen, where one is handling hot food or food containers, and in bathrooms where a mistake in medication levels could harm health or even be life-threatening. So, do not heedlessly reduce light levels without considering your own family needs.

In addition to substituting fluorescent for incandescent lights, you can simply use small bulbs for passage areas where high light levels are not needed. Most room lights give off illumination at nighttime reading levels, which are too high for continuous use. Install dimmer switches in all your rooms, so you can select a light level that is comfortable and safe for any activity. Dimmer switches can not only reduce the amount of electricity you use, but can extend the life of light bulbs, another savings.

LIFESTYLES

The size of your family, their attitudes toward conservation, and their activities play a large part in the amount of energy that you consume. Young children may run in and out from play, especially in very cold weather. The open-door policy can waste much energy and should be discouraged. Ordinary passage going out in the morning to work or school and coming in at night can be enough exposure to promote massive heat loss. Plan to use the least-exposed door as your primary entrance in very cold weather. Reduce air infiltration at doorways by planting shrubs or enclosing porches to shelter them from direct wind.

Using flow control devices on shower heads can reduce the amount of hot water consumed. So, too, will washing full loads of dishes or clothes. When the dishwashing cycle is done, open the door and let the dishes air dry to save electricity. Use cold-water detergents to reduce hot water usage in the laundry, and don't over-dry clothes. Insulate hot water pipes and install an insulation blanket on your water heater.

Lower the thermostat setting on your water heater, and don't forget to lower or turn off the thermostat when you will be gone on vacation or extended trips. Only in America do we pay to heat water when there is no one in the house to use it.

The most crucial energy saver that can be altered by good management is the thermostat. And the more people who tamper with the thermostat, the higher your energy bills will be. If you have older children, sit them down and explain to them that thermostats will be set at an agreed-upon temperature and will not be changed. When I was raising four teenagers, my heating bills were astronomical. What happened was that someone would shut the register in the bathroom to avoid a draft during bathing. Another, feeling cold, would crank up the thermostat. The next might feel a hot-air draft when seated near the wall in the dining room, and shut *that* register. Another would feel cold in his bedroom and crank up his thermostat. The finale of this three-stooges act was when I came home one night, found the thermostat turned to 90 degrees, the furnace burning merrily, and *every* heat register in the house was *closed*. Explain your heating system to the entire family and tell them you alone will handle the thermostat.

Even in my state of Minnesota, you can heat a house in winter to 65 degrees without breaking the bank. But, as you increase that temperature setting by each degree, you will pay a penalty of as much as 3 percent. That means raising the thermostat level by 5 degrees could add a whopping 15 percent or more to your heating bill.

The same is true of air conditioning costs. If you are content with a summertime setting of 80 degrees, and keep windows closed, drapes drawn, and heating appliances such as the stove off, you can minimize air conditioning bills. But, again, each degree of temperature change downward can add 3 percent to your cooling bill. If you choose a thermostat setting of 75 degrees instead of 80 degrees, add 15 percent to your electric bill.

Another thing you can do to cut cooling bills is to dress for the weather while indoors. Cook in the microwave or on the outside barbecue grill to avoid heating up the house. Run all appliances such as laundry equipment at night. Keep light off in rooms that are not occupied, and light occupied rooms sparingly. If you hold your hand near a 75-watt bulb while it is burning (don't touch it, it will burn you!), you will be convinced how much heat each bulb gives off when lit. If you multiply that amount of heat by four or five lights, the heat load is noticeable.

Even the color you choose to decorate your house is significant. Warm, bright colors can make you feel 3 to 4 degrees warmer, according to tests. Conversely, white or other cool colors can make you "feel" as much as 4 degrees colder.

One bit of false advertising: makers of ceiling fans claim they are not only a cooling aid in summer, but that they save energy in winter by helping to circulate warm air. The fact is that moving air makes you feel cooler, whether it is summer or winter, due to the evaporative effect on your skin. And a ceiling fan will not pull hot air from the ceiling downward to warm you. According to the American Ventilating Association undirected air will not "destratify": only the fan motor pulling air through a *duct* can achieve a warming effect in winter. Leave ceiling fans off in cold weather.

CHECKLIST

CONSERVING HOME ENERGY

❑ Check all appliances for energy efficiency before buying. A furnace should have an AFUE rating of at least 80; air conditioners should have a SEER of 10.

❑ Have a professional service technician clean and adjust the burners or standing pilot lights on all gas appliances.

❑ Keep indoor humidity levels between 30 and 60 relative humidity. More humidity can cause mold, mildew, and musty odors; less humidity can make you feel cooler, cause static electricity, loosen joints in woodwork or furniture, and irritate nose and throat membranes.

❑ The least expensive and most regarding energy savings can be found in stopping air infiltration via caulk and weatherstripping of all cracks.

❑ Install dimmer switches to save electricity and lengthen the life of light bulbs.

❑ Turn down every thermostat in the house by a few degrees; each degree above 65°F will add about 3 percent to your winter heating costs. (Turn the air conditioning thermostat up to 80°F in summer.)

❑ Turn down the temperature on your water heater to 110°F. Too hot water can cause severe burns; keeping water temperatures at 140°F or above is wasteful. Put an insulation blanket on your water heater.

❑ Turn off your water heater when going on vacation, even a short trip.

❑ Wash clothes with a cold water detergent to save hot water. Wash only full loads of clothes.

❑ Don't over-dry clothes and always dry a full load.

❑ Insulate hot water pipes. Also, insulate cold water pipes so condensation does not form and drip in the basement.

❑ Wash only full loads of dishes in the dishwasher. When dishes are washed, open the washer door and let dishes air dry.

❑ Insulate your basement or foundation. If you have proper attic and wall insulation, 20 percent of your present heat loss is through basement or foundation walls.

❑ Check attic insulation for any voids. Even small breaks in insulation can result in high heat loss. Check insulation around attic access doors, chimneys, and at eaves to be sure insulation is continuous.

❑ Check attic ventilation. Look in the attic on a cold day: any frost on the underside of your roof deck indicates that moisture is not being properly vented out of the attic. Have a ventilation contractor upgrade your ventilation.

13
Alternative Energy

During the present oil crisis we are hearing again the call for use of alternative fuels. It is a siren song and much to be desired, this yearning for an easy solution to our energy crisis and one that would do so in non-polluting fashion. Our problem is that we built a country — even a world — on the premise that fossil fuels were plentiful, cheap, and non-polluting. Oil spills? It's a big ocean, or river, or whatever; that was our premise.

The fact is that our present economy is built upon use of fossil fuels. We have invested billions in finding, reclaiming, processing, transporting, and delivering these fuels. Even assuming that some miraculous alternative fuel was waiting to be found, certainly we have not found it yet, and it would be years or even decades before we could convert our society away from fossil fuel use.

Nor is the solution to our polluting ways to spend more tax dollars on alternative fuel research. It is a convenient fiction that there are alternatives to be had simply by spending enough tax dollars. This view is highly provincial. There are many countries in the world, rich countries, desperate for alternative fuel sources. Germany, Japan, and Israel are among the nations that would develop alternatives if they could; all consume vast amounts of imported energy, none has domestic fuel in any quantity. I have spoken, at various building trade shows, to members of the Tokyo press, who attended our shows to find, among other things,

what new developments there might be in alternative fuels and energy conservation. It is chauvinistic to proclaim that the rest of the world awaits only the actions of the U.S. president to rescue them from their energy dilemmas. If solar energy, for example, were readily workable with today's technology, we would all be buying solar with labels stamped "Honda" or "Mitsubishi."

Our only alternatives to oil are other fossil fuels such as natural gas and coal. Natural gas is reportedly a clean alternative fuel, with several centuries' supply in known reserves. Coal, of course, has widely been attacked as a source of air pollution and acid rain in its most polluting form; protesters have forced many industries to stop burning coal. But the U.S. is coal-rich, with reserves of coal energy that rival the energy reserves of Saudi Arabia. Might we not find better emission control devices to clean the coal smoke and free ourselves from dependence on foreign oil, or will we surrender to the marchers and forgo consumption of this national treasure?

OIL SHORTAGES

Let us first point out that there is not now, nor has there ever been, a global oil shortage. At the time of the Iraqi invasion of Kuwait, the Saudi oil minister was arguing with U.S. oil representatives against the possibility of the U.S. developing more domestic reserves, because Arab oil exists in known quantities sufficient to supply the world for decades into the future.

When U.S. leaders and oil companies discussed the oil crisis of the early '70s they were speaking of *proven reserves*. Proven reserves refer to discovered oil resources, and mean that we know the oil is there, and we can recover it with present technology. That technology today is far ahead of the technologies of even a decade ago. Satellites search for oil and find it in remote areas; political climates change, and our oil people now are discussing oil exploration in Russia and China; we can drill deeper, even horizontally, with new tools. In addition, steam, natural gas, and other agents can be pumped into oil wells and thus increase recovery rates immensely.

The December 1989 issue of *Oil and Gas Journal* estimated proven world oil reserves to exceed *one trillion barrels*. That is enough oil to last to the year 2040, even if we factor in a worldwide daily increase in consumption of one million barrels per day. We also know that there are large quantities of oil, worldwide, waiting to be discovered. Any shortage of oil is due to restrictions on oil exploration and production, not to any scarcity.

SOLAR ENERGY

In the late '70s I was privileged to visit the first totally integrated solar house in the U.S. News people from all areas of the media were invited to Evansville, Indiana to visit a house built by the Arkansas/Louisiana Gas Co. or ARKLA. The house was built to be as energy efficient as was possible, considering the materials and techniques available at the time. The solar equipment was built entirely by ARKLA and was an active solar system in which water heated in solar collectors was circulated and distributed by a number of pumps, pipes, and conversion units. A 1500-gallon water tank, buried under the driveway, stored the

collected solar energy. The air conditioning was also solar; ARKLA had early experience in converting heat to cold with its gas-burning Servel refrigerators.

Also at the site were people from the newly-formed Department of Energy. I interviewed the DOE people and ARKLA engineers at some length. The building techniques shown were quite remarkable in their ingenuity: super-insulation, framing that permitted wrap-around thermal blankets, 2 X 6 studding for extra insulation thickness, and increased attic insulation were all there, well ahead of the code increases that were later demanded for housing.

In that year the ARKLA project was projected to have a payback period of perhaps seventeen to twenty years. It was a revelation to me that no one who was knowledgeable on the subject expected that solar energy was the magic answer that the media was trumpeting it to be. Each of the technical people I talked to, both from the company (ARKLA) and from the government (DOE), spoke of very modest expectations for solar. When I pressed them on solar's future, most thought that solar might, at best, contribute 5 percent of the nation's energy needs by the year 2000.

The problem with solar energy is one of storage. Annually, enough solar energy falls on the roof of your house to run some 600 homes, by 1980 estimates. The problem is how to store the energy until it is needed. The best storage media we could find in those early times were either water — the medium used by ARKLA — or rocks, which were used in some hot air solar applications. Not very advanced storage mediums, but nothing very spectacular has happened in the search for good storage systems in the last ten years.

The 1500 gallons of water in the ARKLA house were projected to heat the house through perhaps (depending on the temperature) three cloudy days. All solar houses were expected to have backup heating systems to carry the needs through those sunless periods. Solar energy was never, regardless of the rosy reports the media was projecting, considered by knowing people to be a viable alternative to fossil fuels.

Solar energy has some applications in narrow geographical bands. To operate on solar you must have nearly endless sunny days, an extremely efficient thermal shell in the exterior of your house, and live in an area of moderate winter temperatures. For heating water, solar works best when large quantities of water are needed. Solar water heating can be affordable (depending on a number of other variables) for car washes, restaurants, hospitals, or other businesses that need large amounts of hot water. For the home, water heating is best accomplished by current methods.

Another drawback for solar heating is that houses must be extremely energy efficient, designed for solar, before solar becomes practical. It cannot be used at all, with current technology, as a retrofit for existing housing, as existing housing is too inefficient.

As this is written, a solar car has just climbed Pike's Peak; emergency roadside telephones in San Diego County in California are solar-powered. So, for example, are wrist watches and other small gadgets that need little power. But the solar engine that will replace the diesel engine in an eighteen wheeler, power a 747, or light New York City is still a distant dream, and we should not be lulled into thinking that sunshine will meet our tremendous power needs anytime in the foreseeable future.

The idea that we have not thrown enough money at the energy problem is not true. We have spent (the federal government) several billions of dollars on solar research. What we have found is that solar is an extremely expensive, unreliable, and undependable energy source, and that the total possible solar energy production would be minuscule at best. If solar energy were a viable option, the world would not wait upon the U.S. government to pursue it. If solar energy were viable, it would be a reality.

WIND AND TIDE

In the 1970s and since, there has been experimentation with the tides and wind to extract energy from these natural forces. For wind, Pacific Gas and Electric buys power from windmills that were built in Altamount Pass at Livermore, California. However, wind is not a sufficient source of power in most parts of the world, and at best is inefficient due to variable wind velocity. The huge windmills are noisy as well as large, which makes them undesirable in or near urban areas.

There are obvious geographical limitations to tidal power. Many of us do not live within generating distance of the seas. Even for cities located on the seashores, tidal power generation is very expensive and the tides themselves are unpredictable. In addition to geographical limitations, tidal power generators are very expensive to harness.

TRANSPORTATION

I recently have had need to travel a good deal. The entire nation is covered by a network of freeways that permit us to travel with speed and ease anywhere in the U.S. When I hear of alternatives to gasoline-fueled cars, I wonder how we would set up a fuel distribution system as low-cost and as universally available as our system of gasoline service stations. A friend who is an automotive writer visited us in the 1970s. He drove a Pontiac car that had been converted to run on propane. The propane tank filled the car's trunk and left no room for luggage or tools. But the car still retained its gasoline tank and carburetor. When I questioned my friend about this he told me that it was difficult or impossible to find fuel for a propane refill in most cities. We are left with the questions: first, what is the new miracle fuel going to be? How long would it take to set up a nationwide service network so I could drive my car to Disneyland or other vacation points, while being sure of easily accessible fuel outlets? And, if non-fossil substitutes are found, what do we do with the billions of dollars worth of cars and trucks we already have, the vehicles that would become obsolete the day we adopt a substitute?

I recently viewed a TV show in which a young man was earnestly proposing that cars that could run 100 miles per gallon of gas were easily attainable, and that the government has only to command the auto companies to build such a vehicle. That of course is pure hogwash: there is only so much energy in a gallon of gasoline. After you have reached a reasonably efficient burn rate for the fuel, mpg rates are governed by:

1. the weight of the vehicle, and

2. the speed at which you wish to move it.

Even then, the limits of miles per gallon are very limited (by the amount of energy contained in the gallon of fuel). My friend who drives an 800-pound motorcycle reports that he gets about 45 miles per gallon. If auto companies could build a one or two passenger vehicle that weighed only 800 pounds, would you buy it? And, if you bought it, would you like to travel cross-continent in the thing? To be useful, a vehicle has to meet certain minimum standards, among which is the ability to transport two or more people in reasonable safety and comfort and at some reasonable speed.

The same objections are true for the proposed electric cars. Those cars are hardly an original idea: electric-powered cars were tried when internal combustion cars were first built. The internal combustion car won out because it was far superior to electric cars in every way, and it still is. How would we generate enough electricity to power a fleet of cars? Is there some non-polluting way to generate that needed electricity? And do we want

cars that can be driven only short distances, then must be plugged into a recharging unit for hours before we can continue our journey?

There may be a technological breakthrough somewhere in the future that would open entirely new possibilities for energy. So far as any of us know, that breakthrough is far away, if indeed it exists. We cannot live today as though there really were some viable alternatives to what we are doing, because there are not. All forms of alternative energy are today experimental, and taken together would make no dent in our energy demands.

Yet there are those who talk of alternative energy as though it already were reality. They point to a few windmills, a small solar project, and the advances in gasoline mileage we have made over the last decade as though quadrupling those gains is a simple matter of will power. We have already adopted fuel injection, weight reduction, and aerodynamic styling to achieve present fuel efficiency levels. For the short term at least, meaningful gains in miles per gallon will come as a result of downsizing cars. There are already some twenty cars available, at reasonable prices, that get 40 miles per gallon of gas or more. It appears only a small portion (5 percent) of the public wants such vehicles, because they account for only a small percent of sales.

Other industrial nations, such as Germany and Japan, maintain growing economies while consuming about half as much energy per capita as we do. There is no doubt that we waste much of our energy, but the per capita figures are somewhat misleading. We are a vast and sprawling country whose economic base is built around building, driving, and fueling automobiles. We cannot, without dire economic consequences, suddenly abandon our entire economic and social structure.

Would it not be a better approach to face the fact that we have built our nation upon the presumption that fossil fuels would provide our energy, and that it is late in the game to alter that course with any degree of haste? Could we not agree that any changes cannot be done abruptly, and that an alternative to present practice would be phased in over a period of years or decades?

For the present, recycling and conservation offer very real possibilities. It seems more realistic to concentrate our efforts on greater citizen awareness, conservation, and recycling than to engage in a search for unproven alternatives. Research into more efficient emissions controls and filters might prove more rewarding than research money spent to develop electric cars.

CHECKLIST
ALTERNATIVE ENERGY

Do you know:

❑ That it takes almost as much energy (in BTUs) to produce a gallon of ethanol as is *contained* (in BTUs) in a gallon of ethanol? Proponents do not tell us that this "alternative fuel" requires 90,000 BTUs of heat to get a gallon of ethanol that offers only 120,000 BTUs of energy.

❑ That 2/3 of all oil wells in the world are in the U.S.? (Of *913,060* producing oil wells in 1988, *612,448* were American, according to *Oil and Gas Journal*.)

❑ That the average electric car today will run only sixty miles before needing an eight-hour pause to recharge the batteries? That even small electric cars need 800 pounds of lead-acid batteries, while small delivery vans may need a half-ton or more of batteries? That such batteries are a major source of pollution because both acid and lead are hazardous?

❑ That the owner of an electric car may have to dispose of a half-ton of batteries after two to three years, at a cost of $1,000?

❑ What fuel is used for electricity generated in your area? Power plants in my area (Minneapolis) are fired by coal or nuclear power.

❑ That state and federal tax subsidies for ethanol are equal to $1 per gallon for all the ethanol produced since 1979, for a whopping $4.2 billion subsidy total?

❑ That NASA orbiting satellites have found not one degree of "global warming" over the last decade?

❑ That more than 90 percent of existing housing is too poorly constructed (as far as thermal efficiency), badly sited, or geographically undesirable to ever use solar power?

14
The Next Generation

As parents and grandparents, it is not enough to take responsibility for ourselves and our community by beginning home recycling programs. We must do more. We must instill in our children and grandchildren the belief that they have the power to make a difference — a difference in the quality of life on our planet for their generation and generations to come.

If your children ask, "Is recycling really worth the trouble?" the answer is an unequivocal YES. A ton of recycled paper saves about seventeen trees, 7,000 gallons of water, and enough energy to heat the average home for six months. *All* recycling reduces air and water pollution.

Start by setting a good example, then get your children involved. At times you may find it hard to weigh the advantages of one product over another, one type of packaging over another. But don't give up your efforts. As manufacturers, packagers, distributors, and retail outlets realize how much their future sales depend on appropriate, environmentally-friendly packaging, more and more of the "right" options will become not only available but prevalent.

"The first educator, however, is the family, where the child learns to respect his neighbor and to love nature."

Pope John Paul II on the environment "Message to the Universe," *Mother Earth News*

SETTING THE EXAMPLE

Begin right away, by setting the best example you know how. With the help of this book, you have the ideas and tools you need to get started on a comprehensive home recycling, energy-saving program. The sooner you start bundling newspapers and sorting glass, the sooner your children will realize its importance. Explain what you're doing as you go along. Tell your children how recycling newspaper saves not only trees but water and energy; how recycling certain plastics as well as the oil from the car saves petroleum and reduces air pollution and potential groundwater pollution.

GETTING STARTED

Find out the standards for recycling in your area. Some materials (newspaper, glass, aluminum) will be accepted at almost any recycling station. Other materials, including plastics type 1 and 2 (soda bottles and milk jugs, respectively), metal cans, and magazines, are accepted at selected sites. Still other materials, mainly the plastics type 3 through 7 (vinyl, low-density polyethylene, polypropylene, and others) are less widely accepted.

Don't forget to remove the bottle caps and metal rings from glass jars. Glass items should also be rinsed before recycling.

ESTABLISH A RECYCLING ROUTINE

Start a routine for you and your children to follow every week. Kids are great at crushing gallon milk jugs and stamping on aluminum cans. Young children can be responsible for sorting the least hazardous items — newspapers, milk jugs — into recycling bins or boxes. Older children can handle the sharp-edged items, rinsing and sorting the cans and glass items, as well as tying up the stacks of newspaper or putting them in paper grocery bags. If you have potential entrepreneurs in your family, encourage your kids to collect aluminum cans and sell them for cash to a scrap metal dealer. (Aluminum brings the highest price per pound. Other recyclables require too much bulk to achieve any worthwhile profit.)

Recycling can be a game. Have young children take a magnet and use it to determine whether cans are steel or aluminum. The magnet will adhere to the steel cans but not to the aluminum.

PRECYCLING

Don't forget to encourage precycling. Kids of any age can help you determine the most environmentally-friendly packaging, size, etc. Have them look for items that can be recycled, refilled or, at the very least, are packaged in the largest size available. Point out examples of poor packaging — the toy taped to a piece of cardboard three times its size, then blister-packed in non-recyclable plastic. Make a game of looking for these items and their best-packaged (or non-packaged!) counterparts.

If your children are old enough to do some of the shopping for you, make sure they use canvas shopping bags for packing the groceries or take used paper shopping bags and use them again.

GARDENING

Most children love seeing something they've planted grow and flourish, perhaps even bear fruit. If you have the space, offer each child a small garden plot in which to plant flower and vegetable seeds, herb plants (especially the fragrant ones like lemon balm and peppermint), and maybe even a dwarf fruit tree (choose one that is self-pollinating). Encourage the children to help you with the compost — dumping in kitchen waste, turning the pile as needed. Kids will love to have the responsibility of monitoring the lawn's water intake. They can also make simple bird feeders and bird houses to attract these natural predators of the insect population. Write:

Recycle for the Birds
National Wildlife Federation
8925 Leesburg Pike
Alexandria, VA 22184

WATER CONSERVATION

Post a list of good water-use habits in the bathroom. Remind your children not to let the water run and to use cold water for hand-washing whenever possible. You may even want to offer an incentive to those who take shorter showers and monitor leaking faucets. Teach older boys and girls how to change faucet washers.

START A RECYCLING CLUB

Have children start a Recycling Club in the neighborhood. Such a club could include periodic tours of the neighborhood or a local park, picking up all trash. The "trash" could then be sorted into recyclables and actual trash. Come up with projects for the found items, such as making a 2-liter soda bottle into a bird feeder. Discuss other ways to use the seemingly unusable trash.

TEACHING RECYCLING IN OUR SCHOOLS

Try to get your local school system involved in teaching recycling as part of the science curriculum. In Virginia, one organization, Charlottesville Albemarle Recycle Together (CART), approached the city and county school superintendents with an outline of a program on recycling. Directed mainly to kindergarten through fifth graders, their efforts are based on the three R's — reduction, reuse, and recycling. Volunteers from the group present assemblies and instigate recycling programs within the schools. A number of techniques are used to educate the students, including a game show called "Wheel of Recycling." The youngest children play "Go Fish" with magnets and cans. Second and third graders have a relay race to see which team can dismantle and correctly sort a "mini landfill" the fastest.

Teacher participation and encouragement seem to be key to the success of an in-school recycling program. Days are set for the children to bring in their recyclable materials. The education program has tapped support in the business community as well. A local garbage company hauls the recyclables; a soft-drink bottler provides large drums for collecting them.

According to Angela Glomm, CART President, the children's concerns are focused mainly on three areas:

1. Trash pollutes water and can kill marine life;

2. Trash is litter; and

3. Our landfills are filling up.

This last point is illustrated best by the mini-landfill created on the stage during assemblies. The children are asked whether they would like this trash dumped in *their* backyards, and why not?

Most important, the students who have been part of the program are putting their new knowledge to work. In one two-month period in 1990, they collected more than 4,000 pounds of aluminum cans!

RESOURCES

P-3 is an "earth-based" magazine especially for kids. Written for kids ages seven to twelve, it is a colorful thirty-two page journal. A one-year subscription (ten issues) is $14.

P-3
P.O. Box 52
Montgomery, VT 05470

A paper recycling kit is a great way to show kids how paper is made and how they can recycle it themselves. This kit, for ages nine and up, includes screens, sponge, press bar, and blotter paper for making simple pieces of recycled paper. The kit includes the book, *Paper by Kids* (hardbound, 108 pages). About $25.

The "De-light" is a rubber cartoon-like character that fits over any standard light switch and has a 12-inch handle, so children as young as eighteen months can turn lights on and off without help. A great and fun way to teach kids about saving electricity. Set of two, about $8.

The above items (including subscriptions to *P-3*) are available from:

Seventh Generation
Colchester, VT 05446-1672
(800) 456-1177

BOOKS FOR KIDS AND THEIR PARENTS

About Garbage and Stuff
Ann Zane Shanks (New York: Viking Press)

Child's Play: 200 Instant Crafts and Activities for Preschoolers
Leslie Hamilton (New York, Crown Publishers, Inc.)

Ecology: A Practical Introduction with Projects and Activities
Usborne Science and Experiments

50 Simple Things Kids Can Do to Save the Earth
The Earth Works Group (Berkeley, CA: Earthworks Press)

Garbage! Where It Comes From, Where It Goes
Evan and Janet Hadingham (New York: Simon & Schuster)

A Kid's Guide to How to Save the Planet
Billy Goodman (New York: Avon Books)

The Kids' Environment Book: What's Awry and Why
Anne Pedersen (Santa Fe: John Muir Publications)

Let's Grow: 72 Gardening Adventures with Children
Linda Tilgner

Recycling Resources
Laurence Pringle (New York: Macmillan)

Recyclopedia: Games, Science Equipment, and Crafts from Recycled Materials
Robin Simons (Boston: Houghton Mifflin)

What Happens to Garbage?
Rona Beame (New York: Messner)

Conclusion

Most thinking people are disturbed by the mountain of trash that threatens to bury us, and by the pollution of the world and its elements. Equally disturbing is the trend toward exaggeration of the problem, of dire claims that cannot be substantiated. We need, to the extent possible, to learn the truth and to deal with it. Less than the truth, or exaggeration, however motivated, leads us to direct our efforts toward chasing rainbows. Often, these who predict imminent doom ask: "So what if we are wrong? The worst we can do is have a cleaner world, even if we are wrong." Misdirecting our efforts can lead us into habits that are even more damaging than present practices. Well-meaning errors waste available government funds, drive up the cost of living, wreck industries and lives, and reduce our standard of living.

Already, legislation that demands better gas mileage and less pollution from cars has made cars very expensive. The Clean Air Act recently passed has been estimated to cost each citizen — man, woman and child — at least $500 in added cleanup costs. Will it be worth it? If you have seen the blackened forests and dead lakes of eastern Europe, caused by their burning high-sulphur coal, you can see the outcome of massive and unaddressed pollution. But we should not go wildly about, forcing changes that have dire economic and career consequences, without understanding fully what we are about.

For example, we are almost daily warned about the greenhouse effect on the ozone layers at both poles. This destruction of the ozone layers is claimed to be the direct result of our use of fluorocarbons and carbon dioxide. Yet a ten-year study by NASA showed *no warming* over the last ten years. In addition, S. Fred Singer, a professor of environmental sciences at the University of Virginia and director of the U.S. weather satellite program, was reported to believe that if there is a problem with global warming, no one knows or understands from available data what could be causing the warming or what the cure might be. Also, no one knows whether any present emissions, of any kind or from any source, are having an effect on the upper atmosphere. Would it be prudent to reduce waste emissions by whatever levels possible, without destroying major parts of our economy? Certainly it would. Does it make sense to go wildly thrashing about, acting on unsubstantiated information? It does not. We are dealing with people's lives, and ill-informed action can be dangerous — at least as dangerous as inaction.

One small example will suffice. Early in the days of the '70s oil crisis I saw the results of a badly executed urea formaldehyde insulation job. Holes were bored in the exterior (stucco) finish of a house, which reduced the appearance of the exterior and reduced the home's value. Plus, the badly installed insulation was so full of voids — I had to remove some interior plaster soon after the job was insulated — as to be totally worthless as far as any improvement in energy conservation. So I protested to my boss, the editor of a home improvement magazine, that we should not advise people to use foam-in urea formaldehyde insulation. But it was all the rage, and we, along with most of the media, trumpeted the benefits of this action. Only years later, with thousands of houses ruined or damaged, did we all wake to the realization that:

1. the insulation was worthless at best; and

2. that the formaldehyde content made it a health hazard to young children or chemically sensitive persons.

The upshot was that the same governments and media that had urged the citizens to use the stuff then made it illegal to install it. This is the type of hasty, ill-informed action that I fear on the subject of recycling.

Want another example? Take wood-burning. The alternative to fossil fuels (one of them) would be a return to those nostalgic days of yesteryear, when grandpa went to the woods and cut firewood to heat his home. Some of us, old enough to have remembered the drawbacks of those good old days, predicted that this movement would be short-lived. First, when we cut wood in the old days, each home had a woodlot in which to cut, or at least there was such a woodlot nearby. Next, cutting, hauling, stacking, drying, and storing wood is a messy and cumbersome business, aside from being hard work. Also, when we burned wood for fuel, we were farmers or tradesmen who were home all day, to tend those wood fires. So how did the wood-burning revolution fare?

A reader of my magazine wrote me a letter in which he tried to show the true cost of burning wood. After extolling the value of the exercise it took to cut, stack, and carry the stuff, he got down to the hidden costs. These included a 4-wheel-drive vehicle to haul the wood home from the forest; expensive chain saws and splitters to work up the wood; paying for fire and smoke damage when his house caught fire, and the ensuing legal costs of the divorce which his wife got. All told, the gentlemen estimated that burning wood had cost him about $150,000 in that fiscal year, which numbers did not include future payments for alimony and child support.

Setting aside any attempts to see a humorous side to our periodic flights from sanity, the reality is that burning wood is polluting (second only to burning coal in emissions), messy, hard work, and hazardous to your health. Studies have estimated that children who inhabit homes where wood is burned have twice as many respiratory ailments as those children whose homes feature wall-hung thermostats.

CAN I MAKE A DIFFERENCE?

A basic assumption for a democratic society is that the citizen will take the trouble to inform himself or herself and to act on his or her own perceived best interests. It requires some effort on the part of the citizen to do this, because a wide variety of politicians, industries, unions, and others spend much money and time trying to get you to vote *against* your own best interests, or at least for *their* best interests. It is because people in a democracy need to be informed to decide their own interests that the First Amendment rights to a free press were established. People must have access to information to vote sensibly.

Among politicians, Teddy Roosevelt made a difference, because he helped establish our national parks. Much later, another politician, Senator Gaylord Nelson, made a difference, when he conceived the idea of an Earth Day. I think Lady Bird Johnson, as First Lady, made a difference with her program for highway beautification. After these three, it is difficult to list many political leaders, or a political party, that can claim a better record, and we should be very cautious about whom we elect, simply on their claim of being "greener" than their opponent.

Who can we turn to? If memory serves, governors of both parties have stood watch while California redwood forests were converted to picnic tables. Boston Harbor is highly polluted, as are the beaches of the Atlantic and Pacific. A recent news story reported of beaches being closed in California because sewer outlets were thoughtfully positioned to dump on beaches used for bathing. The acid rain of northern lakes and pollution upon nearly every river in the country are not the result of actions of one political party.

It is a good rule of thumb never to vote for any politician who arrives in a 4-wheel-drive vehicle, or wears stone-washed blue jeans, unless he also wears blue jeans in his legislative office.

Take oil pollution. Most of the major disasters with oil spills are the result of tanker accidents, along the lines of *Exxon Valdez*. Off-shore and pipeline oil spills can be limited and/or contained (the fact that they sometimes are *not* so contained should be a matter of government enforcement, not policy). Yet the politicians who denounced Exxon had an opportunity to vote that Alaska oil be transported by pipeline, and they chose to bring it out by tanker, unquestionably the potentially most dangerous way to move it. In the aftermath of the spill we heard Congress debate about mandating double-hulled, unsinkable tankers. The tankers would cost about $90 million each more to build, double-hulled. For those who believe that is the answer, I know where we can buy plans, cheap, for an unsinkable ship. The ship was *Titanic*. Yesterday, today, and tomorrow, elderly rustbucket tankers flying foreign flags dock at our ports. These ships could not, by any stretch of the imagination, pass our own Coast Guard standards. The disaster potential is overwhelming, and we should address it. Is any politician doing so?

As might be seen, I have little confidence that the federal government will act. I also believe that massive action breeds massive mistakes. There are enough examples, in every state in the Union, to warrant my skepticism.

The argument that only national action will save our country or planet ignores the fact that some states have achieved great results by their own actions: some cities are light years ahead of others. This is due to citizen involvement and government action at the source of the problem. We do not need any president's permission to clean up our own city or state, and if a significant number of us cared enough to become informed we could change a nation.

I am not unaware of the fact that some problems are national in scope. I for one would be willing to let oil companies drill wherever there is oil, on the condition that they use the best technology available to avoid damaging the land, and on the further condition that our federal laws were tough enough to punish, or even order the breakup of, those companies that willfully implemented less than the best safeguards available to prevent pollution.

We already have in place an energy delivery system that is the best in the world. A two-pronged approach that would deal with conservation and safe handling/transport of fossil fuels, with severe punishment to ban the willful and the greedy from business, would go far to reduce our disposal and pollution problems. It is not a solution to demand electric cars while opposing construction of new electrical generating facilities.

As I read of the efforts of conservation and recycling, I read of 75 percent participation in recycling programs in the city of St. Louis Park, Minnesota; of growing success with recycling in Seattle, Washington, in San Francisco, California, and throughout the state of Maine. Can it be done? I think the obvious answer is yes. Does it require the federal government to begin massive new programs, both spending and legislating? I think the answer has proven to be no. The answer may be found in Robert Fulghum's book of kindergarten basics: If you made the mess, you are the logical one to clean it up.

Appendices

Books, Magazines, and Resources
Organizations
Manufacturers and Catalogs

BOOKS, MAGAZINES, AND RESOURCES

"The Art of Composting" (brochure)
Metropolitan Service District
2000 S.W. 1st Avenue
Portland, OR 97201
(503) 221-1646

"Bagging the Great Paper vs Plastic Debate" (free article)
National Audubon Society
950 Third Avenue
New York, NY 10022

Better Planet Books
P.O. Box 1263
Montpelier, VT 05601

BioCycle: Journal of Waste Recycling
P.O. Box 351
Emmaus, PA 18049
(215) 967-4135

Coming Full Circle: Successful Recycling Today
($20.00)
Environmental Defense Fund
257 Park Avenue South
New York, NY 10010
(212) 505-2100

The Complete Book of Home Environmental Hazards, by Roberta Altman ($24.95)
Facts on File
460 Park Avenue South
New York, NY 10016
(800) 322-8755

Complete Trash: The Best Way to Get Rid of Practically Everything Around the House, by Norm Crampton
Little, Brown & Co.
200 West Street
Waltham, MA 02154
(800) 343-9204
(617) 890-0250

Conscious Consumer Newsletter
700 N. Milwaukee Avenue
Vernon Hills, IL 60061

The Consumer's Energy Handbook, by Peter Norback and Craig Norback
Van Nostrand Reinhold
115 Fifth Avenue
New York, NY 10003
(212) 254-3232

Cut Your Electric Bills in Half, by Ralph J. Herbert
($16.95 or $9.95 paperback)
Rodale Press Inc.
Distributed by:
St. Martin's Press Inc.
175 Fifth Avenue
New York, NY 10010
(800) 221-7945

Directory of State Environmental Agencies ($22.50)
Environmental Law Institute
1718 Connecticut Avenue NW, Suite 300
Washington, DC 20036
(202) 232-7933

Environment
Heldreff Publications
4000 Albemarle Street NW
Washington, DC 20016
(202) 362-6445

50 Simple Things You Can Do to Save the Earth,
by The Earth Works Group ($4.95)
Earthworks Press
P.O. Box 25
Berkeley, CA 94709

Garbage: The Practical Journal for the Environment
435 Ninth Street
Brooklyn, NY 11215
(718) 788-1700

The Global Ecology Handbook: What You Can Do About the Environmental Crisis
Beacon Press
25 Beacon Street
Boston, MA 02108
(617) 742-2110

Greenpeace Paper Book ($3.00)
Also: "White Wash: The Dioxin Cover-Up" (free article)
Greenpeace
4649 Sunnyside Avenue, North
Seattle, WA 98103
(206) 632-4326

Guide to Hazardous Products Around the Home ($9.95)
Household Hazardous Waste Project
Southwest Missouri State University
901 South National Avenue, Box 108
Springfield, MO 65804
(417) 836-5777

Healthy House: How to Buy One, How to Build One, How to Cure a "Sick" One, by John Bower ($17.95)
Carol Publishing Group
120 Enterprise Avenue
Secaucus, NJ 07094
(201) 866-8159

Heloise: Hints for a Healthy Planet ($7.95)
Putnam Publishing Group
200 Madison Avenue
New York, NY 10016
(800) 631-8571

The Home Energy Decision Book, by Gigi Coe, Michael Garland, and Michael Eaton ($9.95)
Sierra Club Books
Orders to:
Random House Inc.
201 E. 50th Street
New York, NY 10022
(800) 726-0600
(212) 751-2600

"Home Safe Home" (A chart of alternative household cleaners; $1.00)
Clean Water Fund
New Jersey Environmental Federation
808 Belmar Plaza
Belmar, NJ 07719
(201) 280-8988

Home Safe Home: How to Make Your Home Environmentally Safe, by William J. Kelly
National Press Inc.
7200 Wisconsin Avenue, Suite 212
Bethesda, MD 20814
(800) 622-6657
(301) 657-1616

Homeowner's Guide to Saving Energy, by Billy L. Price and James T. Price
TAB Books Inc.
Blue Ridge Summit, PA 17214
(800) 233-1128

Household Waste: Issues and Opportunities
Concern Inc.
1794 Columbia Road NW
Washington, DC 20009
(202) 328-8160

How to Make the World a Better Place, by Jeffrey Hollender ($19.95 or $9.95 paperback)
William Morrow & Co., Inc.
105 Madison Avenue
New York, NY 10016
(800) 843-9389
(212) 889-3050

How to Re-Use Wastes in Home, Industry and Society, by Jerome Goldstein ($14.95 or $6.95 paperback)
Schocken Books, Inc.
400 Hahn Road
Westminster, MD 21157
(800) 733-3000

Keep America Beautiful Multi-Material Recycling Manual ($25.00)
9 W. Broad Street
Stamford, CT 06902

Let It Rot! The Home Gardener's Guide to Composting, by Stu Campbell ($5.95)
Storey Communications, Inc.
Orders to:
Harper & Row
Keystone Industrial Park
Scranton, PA 18512
(800) 242-7737

The Nontoxic Home, by Debra Dadd
Jeremy P. Tarcher
5858 Wilshire Blvd.
Los Angeles, CA 90036
(213) 935-9980

"Planning for Community Recycling: A Citizen's Guide to Resources" (pamphlet)
Environmental Action
1525 New Hampshire Avenue NW
Washington, DC 20036
(202) 745-4870

Recycling for Living, Fun and Profit ($5.00)
Also: *Recycling Workbook* ($5.95)
Prosperity & Profits
Box 570213
Houston, TX 77257

Recycling Handbook, by Susan Hassol and Beth Richman ($3.95)
Also: *Energy Handbook, Handbook of Everyday Chemicals*
Windstar Foundation
2317 Snowmass Creek Road
Snowmass, CO 81654
(303) 923-2145

Regenerating the Environment: A guide for doers
Community Regeneration
Rodale Institute
222 Main Street
Emmaus, PA 18098

Renew America Report (quarterly newsletter)
Renew America
1400 16th Street NW, Suite 710
Washington, DC 20036

Shopping for a Better Environment, by Laurence Tasaday ($9.95)
Simon & Schuster Inc.
1230 Avenue of the Americas
New York, NY 10020
(800) 223-2348

Shopping for a Better World, by Rosalyn Will ($4.95)
Council on Economic Priorities
20 Irving Place, 9th Floor
New York, NY 10003
(800) 822-6435

The Smart Kitchen, by David Goldbeck ($15.95)
Ceres Press
P.O. Box 87
Woodstock, NY 12498
(914) 679-5573

Toxics, Chemicals, Health, and the Environment,
Lester B. Lave and Arthur C. Upton, editors
($16.50)
Johns Hopkins University Press
Baltimore, MD 21211
(301) 338-6900

War on Waste: Can America win its battle with garbage?, by Louis Blumberg and Robert Gottlieb ($34.95 or $19.95 paperback)
Island Press
P.O. Box 7
Covelo, CA 95428
(800) 828-1302

"Water Efficiency for Your Home" (free booklet)
Rocky Mountain Institute
1739 Snowmass Creek Road
Snowmass, CO 81654-9199

ORGANIZATIONS

Alliance for Clean Energy
1901 N. Ft. Myer Drive, 12th Floor
Rosslyn, VA 22209
(703) 841-1781
Publishes weekly newsletter.

Alliance to Save Energy
1725 K Street NW, Suite 914
Washington, DC 20036
(202) 857-0666

Aluminum Recycling Association
1000 16th Street NW
Washington, DC 20036
(202) 785-0951

American Council for an Energy-Efficient
Economy
1001 Connecticut Avenue NW, Suite 535
Washington, DC 20036
(202) 429-8873
Publishes booklet: "The Most Energy Efficient
Appliances."

Americans for the Environment
1400 16th Street NW
Washington, DC 20036
(202) 797-6665

Automotive Dismantlers and Recyclers
Association
10400 Eaton Place, Suite 203
Fairfax, VA 22030-2208
(703) 385-1001

Bio-Integral Resource Center
P.O. Box 7414
Berkeley, CA 94707
(415) 524-2567
Publishes *Common Sense Pest Control Quarterly*.

Cause for Concern
R.D. 1, Box 570
Stewartsville, NJ 08886
(201) 479-4110
Publishes quarterly newsletter.

Center for Environmental Information
99 Court Street
Rochester, NY 14604
(716) 546-3796

Citizen's Clearinghouse for Hazardous Waste
P.O. Box 3541
Arlington, VA 22216
(703) 276-7070

Citizens for a Better Environment
33 E. Congress, Suite 523
Chicago, IL 60605
(312) 939-1530
Publishes *Environmental Review* (quarterly).

Environmental Action Coalition
625 Broadway
New York, NY 10012

Environmental Action, Inc.
1525 New Hampshire Avenue NW
Washington, DC 20036
(202) 745-4870

Environmental Hazards Management Institute
10 Newmarket Road
P.O. Box 932
Durham, NC 03824
(603) 868-1496
Distributes the "Recycling Wheel™", "Household
Hazardous Waste Wheel™," and "Water Sense
Wheel."

Greenpeace
4649 Sunnyside Avenue, North
Seattle, WA 98103
(206) 632-4326

Greenpeace Recycling Project
1436 U Street NW
Washington, DC 20009
(202) 462-1177

Household Hazardous Waste Project
901 S. National Avenue
Box 108
Springfield, MO 65804
(417) 836-5777

INFORM
381 Park Avenue South
New York, NY 10016
(212) 689-4040
Publishes *INFORM Reports* (bimonthly).

Institute of Scrap Recycling Industries
1627 K Street NW, Suite 700
Washington, DC 20006
(202) 466-4050

Keep America Beautiful, Inc.
9 West Broad Street
Stamford, CT 06902

Mothers and Others for a Livable Planet
Natural Resources Defense Council
40 West 20th Street
New York, NY 10011
(212) 727-4474

National Audubon Society
950 Third Avenue
New York, NY 10022

National Coalition Against the Misuse of
Pesticides
530 7th Street SE
Washington, DC 20003
(202) 543-5450

National Polystyrene Recycling Company
1025 Connecticut Avenue NW, Suite 508
Washington, DC 20036
(800) 242-7434

National Recycling Coalition
1101 30th Street NW
Washington, DC 20007
(202) 625-6406
Publishes quarterly newsletter.

Plastics Recycling Foundation
1275 K Street NW, Suite 500
Washington, DC 20005
(202) 371-5200

Renew America
1400 16th Street NW, Suite 710
Washington, DC 20036
(202) 232-2252

Resources for the Future
1616 P Street NW
Washington, DC 20036
(202) 328-5000

Rocky Mountain Institute
1739 Snowmass Creek Road
Snowmass, CO 81654-9199

Sierra Club
P.O. Box 7959
San Francisco, CA 94120

The Society of the Plastics Industry, Inc.
1275 K Street, NW, Suite 400
Washington, DC 20005

Steel Can Recycling Association
Foster Plaza X
680 Anderson Drive
Pittsburgh, PA 15220
(412) 922-2772

Waste Watch
P.O. Box 298
Livingston, KY 40445

Wilderness Society
1400 I Street NW
Washington, DC 20005
(202) 842-3400
Publishes *Wilderness* magazine (quarterly).

Worldwatch Institute
1776 Massachusetts Avenue NW
Washington, DC 20036
(202) 452-1999

MANUFACTURERS AND CATALOGS

Advanced Recycling Systems
P.O. Box 1796
Waterloo, IA 50704
(319) 291-6007
Home recycling containers.

AFM Enterprises Inc.
1140 Stacy Court
Riverside, CA 92507
(714) 781-6860
Water-based paints, lacquers, glues; biodegradable
cleaning products.

Alternative Energy Engineering
P.O. Box 339
Redway, CA 95560
Solar equipment.

Amway
(800) 544-7167
Phosphate free, biodegradable cleaning products.

Atlantic Environmental Products Company
(800) 768-1515
Air filter system.

Atlantic Recycled Paper Co.
(800) 323-2811
Recycled paper including copy paper, envelopes,
computer paper, tissues and towels, labels.

Auro Organic Paints
Sinan Co. Natural Building Materials
P.O. Box 181
Suisun City, CA
(707) 427-2325
Paints, lacquers, waxes, cleaners.

The Bag Connection
P.O. Box 817
Newberg, OR 97132
(800) 622-2448
Home recycling container systems.

Barclay Recycling Inc.
(416) 240-8227
Soilsaver® composter.

Bau, Inc.
P.O. Box 190
Alton, NH 03808
(800) 628-8113
(603) 364-2400 in New Jersey
Environmentally safe home products.

Bennett Industries
P.O. Box 519
Peotone, IL 60468
(312) 258-3211

Berner Air Products, Inc.
P.O. Box 5410F
New Castle, PA 16105
Air quality units.

A Brighter Way
P.O. Box 18446
Austin, TX 78760
Compact fluorescent light bulbs.

CHIP Distribution
P.O. Box 704
Manhattan Beach, CA 92507
(714) 781-6860
Concentrated cleaners, non-flammable and
biodegradable.

The Compassionate Consumer
P.O. Box 27
Jericho, NY 11753
(718) 445-4134
Environmentally-friendly cleaning products.

Conservatree Paper Company
10 Lombard Street, Suite 250
San Francisco, CA 94111
(800) 522-9000
Unbleached, 100 percent recycled writing papers.

Co-op America
2100 M Street NW
Washington, DC 20036
(800) 456-1177
Water-saving devices, many other products.

Cycles End
P.O. Box 2350
Durango, CO 81302
Recycled plastic products.

Dalen Products
11110 Gilbert Drive
Knoxville, TN 37932
(615) 966-6404
Composter.

Earth Care Paper Inc.
P.O. Box 3335
Madison, WI 53704
(608) 256-5522
Recycled paper supplies.

Ecco Bella Natural & Ecological Products
6 Provost Square, Suite 602
Caldwell, NJ 07006
(800) 888-5320

Eco Concerns
7007 Carroll Avenue
Takoma Park, MD 20912
(301) 270-0884
Recycled paper products.

Ecological Water Products
1341 W. Main Road
Middletown, RI 02840
(401) 849-4004
Low-flow shower heads, other water-saving devices.

The Energy Store
P.O. Box 3507
Santa Cruz, CA 95063
(800) 288-1938
Lighting, heating and cooling, water conservation items; thermostats and timers; kitchen appliances, more.

Environmental Concerns
9051 Mill Station Road
Sebastopol, CA 95472
(707) 829-7957
(800) 688-8345
Recycled paper products, water filters, lighting products, non-toxic paints, air purification systems.

Franklin Recycling Systems
P.O. Box 708
910 E. Lincoln Avenue
Belvidere, IL 61008
(815) 544-6676
Office recycling systems.

Garden Way Manufacturing
102nd Street & 9th Avenue
Troy, NY 12180
(800) 833-6990
Rotary tillers, other lawn equipment.

Gardener's Supply
128 Intervale Road
Burlington, VT 05401
(800) 533-4551
Gardening, composting supplies.

Good Friends Catalog
1025 W. 8th Street
Kansas City, MO 64101
Cleaning and other products.

Household Recycling Products
P.O. Box 1124
Middleton, MA 01929
(508) 475-1776

IPL Products Ltd.
348 Park Street
North Reading, MA 01864
(508) 664-5595
Home recycling container.

Jade Mountain
P.O. Box 4616
Boulder, CO 80306
(303) 449-6601
Energy-saving light bulbs and fixtures.

Kemp Co.
160 Koser Road
Lititz, PA 17543
Chipper/shredder, other composting supplies.

LewiSystems
128 Hospital Drive
Watertown, WI 53094
(800) 558-9563
Home recycling containers.

Livos PlantChemistry
1365 Rufina Circle
Santa Fe, NM 87501
(505) 438-3448
Non-toxic paints and stains without fumes; cleaning products.

Management Science Applications
123 E. Ninth Street, Suite 204
Upland, CA 91786
(714) 981-0894
Home recycling container systems.

Mantis Manufacturing
1458 County Line Road
Huntingdon Valley, PA 19006
(800) 344-4030
Chipper/shredder.

Microphor, Inc.
452 E. Hill Road
Willits, CA 94590
(707) 459-5563
Home recycling products.

Mulch Trap
Box 8055
Hermitage, TN 37076
(615) 244-8021
A kitchen composting aid, the Mulch Trap fits in standard garbage disposals and diverts shredded organic matter into a compost bucket.

Otto Industries
P.O. Box 410251
Charlotte, NC 28241
(601) 922-0331
Home recycling containers.

Pawnee Products
P.O. Box 751
Goddard, KS 67052
(316) 794-2213
Home recycling containers.

Philadelphia Can Co.
4000 N. American Street
Philadelphia, PA 19140
(215) 223-3500
Recycling systems.

Refuse Removal Systems
P.O. Box 2258
Fair Oaks, CA 95628
(800) 231-2212
Home recycling containers.

Rehrig Pacific Co.
4010 E. 26th Street
Los Angeles, CA 90023
(213) 262-5145

Resource Conservation Technology, Inc.
2633 North Calvert Street
Baltimore, MD 21218
(301) 366-1146
Water-saving toilets, roofing materials, other
building materials.

Resources Conservation, Inc.
P.O. Box 71
Greenwich, CT 06838
(800) 243-2862
Water-saving devices.

Reuter, Inc.
410 11th Avenue S.
Hopkins, MN 55343
(612) 935-6921
Recycling container.

The Ribbon Factory
(702) 736-2484
Offer service of reloading old typewriter ribbons
and laser printer cartridges as well as recycled paper, other supplies.

Ringer Corporation
9959 Valley View Road
Eden Prairie, MN 55344
(612) 941-4180
Chemical-free fertilizers, pesticides, composting
products.

Ropak Atlantic
2B Corn Road
Dayton, NJ 08810
(201) 329-3020
Home recycling system.

Seventh Generation
(800) 456-1177
Recycled paper products, cleaning products,
sorters and recycling cabinets, composter.
Batteries, fluorescent replacement light bulbs,
radon test kit, water-saving products, books, more.

Shaklee
97 Blanchard Road
Cambridge, MA 02138
(617) 547-7600
Natural cleaning products.

Shamrock Industries, Inc.
834 N. 7th Street
Minneapolis, MN 55411
(800) 822-2342
Home recycling containers.

Snyder Industries
P.O. Box 4583
Lincoln, NE 68504
(402) 467-5221
Home recycling container.

Solarcone, Inc.
Box 67
Seward, IL 61077
(815) 247-8454
Cone composting unit constructed of recycled
plastic.

S.O.S. Recycled Paper
Save Our EcoSystems, Inc.
541 Willamette Street, Suite 315
Eugene, OR 97401
(503) 484-2679
Unbleached, 100 percent recycled paper.

Sunrise Lane
780 Greenwich Street
New York, NY 10014
(212) 242-7014
Household cleaning products.

System 1 Filter Systems
1822A E. Main Street
Visalia, CA 93291
(800) 554-3533
(800) 231-9137 in California
Permanent, reusable oil filter for cars.

The Toro Company
Minneapolis, MN 55420
(612) 472-8350
Lawn equipment.

Toter, Inc.
P.O. Box 5338
Statesville, NC 28677
(704) 872-8171
Containers for home recycling.

White Electric Co., Inc.
1511 San Pablo Avenue
Berkeley, CA 94702
(800) 468-2852
Energy-saving light bulbs.

Windsor Barrel Works
P.O. Box 47
Kempton, PA 19529
(800) 527-7848
Receptacles for office recycling.

Write Now
100 North Fifth Street
Lewisburg, PA 17837
(717) 523-0702
Recycled paper products for individual and business use.

Index